# THE SOLSTICE YEARBOOK

A year of rituals, festivals, and ancient magic for modern life

VICTORIA HARRISON

Illustrated by
Lauren Spooner

VERBENA

# Contents

# Introduction

Have you ever felt a rush of energy at Midsummer? Or felt a need to rebalance in the autumn, or a longing to hunker down and light candles at Midwinter? If so you're already answering the call of an ancient solar calendar; one that's been guiding us for centuries and continues to gently shine a path for us to follow, if we know where to look.

Sun worship is one of the oldest practices on earth. We instinctively turn our faces to the sun, we bathe under it, and our cultures were built on the worship of it. Our ancient history is filled with sun gods and goddesses, and our landscapes are peppered with monuments to the solstices and equinoxes dating back thousands of years. But what does this have to do with the way we live today?

Well, actually, quite a lot. We're still deeply solar-powered creatures, whether we realize it or not, and the sun affects everything we do. As we travel through a year, the strength of the sun grows and diminishes, creating our seasons and impacting our moods and energies. Think about how you feel at the height of summer when powered by long hours of sunlight compared to your mood in the depths of winter when you're cocooned in long hours of darkness; the difference can be dramatic.

Our ancestors instinctively understood this power and followed the phases of the sun closely, aligning their lives with the solstices and equinoxes. They built calendars, rituals, and festivals around these key solar dates in the year. In recent times however, many of us have stepped away from a seasonal way of living in a bid to maintain a constant level of productivity all year round. But when we are constantly switched on and active, we can miss the seasonal cues that are trying so clearly to tell us when to rest.

Following a solstice-based calendar helps us to adjust our energies to match the natural world and discover ways to work *with* the phases of the sun, rather than against them.

If you've ever felt out of step with the natural world or stressed with the pace of modern life, finding your way back to a solar calendar can help to weave a slower rhythm back into your year. Everything unfolds at its own gentle pace in the solstice calendar, and daylight hours don't drastically change from one day to the next; instead they increase or decrease slowly by just a few minutes each day, getting longer in the build-up to the Summer Solstice, and then decreasing as we turn towards the Winter Solstice; and this slow and steady turning of the year can be a deeply peaceful rhythm to follow.

Following simple solar rituals can also allow us to pick up threads that link us back to our past. There's ancient magic to be found at every moment in the year, but this is particularly heightened around the time of the equinoxes and solstices, where myths and folklore abound. As we work through this book we'll delve into the mythology and stories of each festival, looking at how they've been celebrated for centuries, as well as seeing what they can teach us about the way we live today. We'll uncover the stories and myths that swirl around them, as well as discovering modern rituals to follow and seasonal crafts to try for each. We'll set intentions at the Spring Equinox, feast under the Midsummer sun, bottle the sun at the Autumn Equinox, and light golden solstice candles at the Winter Solstice.

## WHAT ARE THE SOLSTICES AND EQUINOXES?

In each calendar year there are two solstices (summer and winter) and two equinoxes (autumn and spring). At the solstices, daylight hours are at their maximum or minimum, and at the equinoxes, day and night are of almost equal length.

They occur because the Earth's axis is on a tilt so as it orbits around the Sun over the course of a year, the Earth is either tilted *towards* or *away from* the Sun. This tilt is what dictates the length of our days and creates our seasons.

In the Northern Hemisphere, the Summer Solstice occurs in June when the Earth is at its maximum tilt towards the Sun, creating the longest day and the shortest night of the year. The Winter Solstice occurs in December when the Earth is at its maximum tilt away from the Sun, creating the longest night and the shortest day of the year. The word "solstice" comes from the Latin *sōlstitium*, which translates as *sōl*, (sun) and *sistere*, (to stand still) because during each solstice it appears that the Sun stops still in the sky for a few days.

The equinoxes occur when, for a brief moment, the Sun is directly above the Earth's Equator. At this moment neither Hemisphere is tilted away from *or* towards the Sun, thus creating a day and night of equal length across the globe. The word "equinox" comes from the Latin *equi* (equal) and *nox* (night) which means "equal night".

Because of the Earth's tilt, the Northern Hemisphere and the Southern Hemisphere experience the solstices and equinoxes in opposition. For example, when the Northern Hemisphere is facing fully towards the Sun in June, creating the Summer Solstice, the Southern Hemisphere is tilted away, creating the Winter Solstice, and vice versa.

For the purposes of this book, we will look at how the solstices and equinoxes are experienced in the Northern Hemisphere, but this can be reversed in order to apply to the Southern Hemisphere.

Autumn
Equinox

# What is the Autumn Equinox?

The Autumn Equinox occurs when, for a brief moment, the Sun is directly above the Earth's Equator. At this moment the Earth is tilted neither away from *nor* towards the Sun. This means that during the equinox there will be approximately 12 hours of day and 12 hours of night.

The Autumn Equinox falls between 20 and 24 September, exactly halfway between the Summer Solstice and Winter Solstice. In the Northern Hemisphere, the September equinox marks the astronomical start of autumn.

Directly after the equinox we then start to turn towards the dark half of the year, and each day onwards, the minutes of daylight decrease and the minutes of darkness increase as we head towards the shortest day on the Winter Solstice.

# How Does it Affect Us?

In the cycle of the solar year, the Autumn Equinox is a beautiful moment of balance and warmth, offering the perfect bridge between the light and dark halves of the year, which is why I'm starting with this particular festival. After the intense brightness of the summer months, it can feel as though everything switches into a lower and gentler gear as we approach the equinox; the colours, flavours, and folklore of the season all become deeper and richer as the sun gets lower in the sky. In the natural world, hedgerows begin to quieten, fruit ripens, and plants set seed as migratory birds begin to depart. With the heat and pressure of the summer fading away, the equinox offers us a moment of stillness and calm.

There is something really magical about autumn, and it is without a doubt my favourite season. From the rich colours to the low golden light and the sun-ripened fruit, everything about the equinox is a love letter to the sun. There's an abundance in nature that can happen only at this time of year, thanks to the long hours of warm sunshine that have been poured onto the ground over the summer. Hedgerows and trees are heavy with berries and fruit, leaves blaze orange, yellow, and gold, and there is still plenty of lingering warmth in the air. In the cycle of the year, it's a time of harvesting and gratitude.

Thanks to the equal hours of sunlight and darkness at the equinox, our energy levels should be beautifully balanced right now, which offers us an opportunity to stop and reflect between the extremes of the solstices. If the Spring Equinox is a time for making hopeful plans for the summer ahead, the Autumn Equinox is the time for reflection and gratitude as we look back at the summer and acknowledge everything it's given us. For a moment we are pitched perfectly between the extroverted energy of summer and the introverted energy of winter, and as such, we might experience a grounded sense of calm in ourselves.

After this golden moment of balance, we will then start a gentle shift towards the darker half of the year. For some it's a bittersweet time as we say goodbye to the summer, for others it's a time of purpose and busyness with a sense of preparation and of battening down for the winter months. Although the days have been steadily shortening ever since we tipped past the Summer Solstice back in June, it will really start to become noticeable now, and the decreasing hours of daylight will signal to our bodies that we are entering a phase of rest.



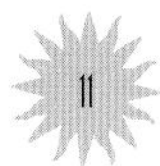

As the natural world around us starts to settle and shift into its autumn colours, we might feel a stilling and settling of energy within ourselves, too, as we respond to the decreasing daylight. With fewer hours of sunlight from the equinox onwards, we will have fewer opportunities to solar charge ourselves during the day, and for many of us, this results in a slow decrease in energy levels from the equinox onwards. As with everything in the solar year though, this is not a sudden or abrupt change, It's a gentle shift. There are still plenty of warm, sunny days for us to enjoy at this time of year, but they begin to be laced with an undertone of woodsmoke and a cooling in the air, signalling a change is coming. We might not be quite ready for hibernation yet, but we are peeking at it over the horizon, starting the process of drawing inwards, taking a deep breath, and letting our shoulders drop as we welcome the start of the cosy season.

After months of hot summer sun, it can be refreshing to be greeted by this cooler weather around the equinox, and for many of us, this is a chance to relax into a slower pace, to stock up our reading pile, and to enjoy the novelty of wearing cosy scarves and sweaters again. Perhaps even to light the first fire of the season. But while some of us relish this change in energy, others can struggle with this seasonal shift and feel anxious about the move towards the darker half of the year. This is why it's crucial to understand our own personal response to the season and to give ourselves time to adjust to it if required.

At this quieting time of the year, we might need to take on less in terms of work or social commitments, for example, to allow ourselves time to settle and rest. Or we might need to ensure we take regular walks outside during the hours of daylight to solar charge ourselves.

We might want to take part in a ritual to mark the shift in season or treat ourselves to the best seasonal foods we can find: anything that helps to reframe the season and treat our bodies to some well needed rest after a busy summer season.

Approached in the right way, the Autumn Equinox should feel like a soft and gentle turn towards the dark, like sinking into a comfortable armchair after a long and productive day.

THE AUTUMN EQUINOX IS THE TIME FOR REFLECTION AND GRATITUDE AS WE LOOK BACK AT THE SUMMER AND ACKNOWLEDGE EVERYTHING IT'S GIVEN US

# Ancient Magic and Folklore of the Autumn Equinox

No season is fuller of romance and magic than autumn. It's a time of woodsmoke, folktales, and, of course, glorious colour. As with any moment in the year when a change in solar energy occurs, there's a spiritual and liminal quality to this time, a sense of being on the boundary between worlds, which can be seen in the eerie folktales and myths of the autumn season. Poised exactly between the Summer and Winter Solstices, the moment of equilibrium offered by the Autumn Equinox can also be seen as a chance to take stock and rebalance.

While there aren't as many clues as to how our ancestors celebrated this time of year as there are at the solstices, there are still indicators that this was a time of spiritual and practical importance to previous civilizations. Ancient monuments to sun worship at the equinox, for example, can be found all over the world. Although the exact purpose of many of these monuments remains shrouded in mystery, the precise engineering that allows them to line up perfectly with the rising sun on the equinox would indicate the importance of this day to the civilizations that built them.

At Loughcrew in Ireland, for example, a series of passage tombs dating back to the Neolithic period hold a particular equinox mystery. Twice a year at sunrise, on each equinox, a beam of rising sunlight travels down the passage of one of these tombs, to shine directly on the Stone Age symbols carved on the back stone. This demonstrates not only a precise understanding of a solar calendar by an ancient civilization but also their ability of work with the sun to engineer a beautiful and spiritual monument to their loved ones and ancestors.

In the ancient Inca city of Machu Picchu in Peru the *Intihuatana* stone, the name of which translates as "the place to tie up the sun", draws visitors every equinox. This stone monument has four sides facing North, South, East, and West and appears to be precisely engineered in order to act as an early sundial or solar calendar. The stone casts a shadow throughout the year in the manner of a sundial, except for at two precise moments. At noon on each of the equinoxes, when the sun sits directly above the stone, the shadow completely disappears. Effectively the sun has been "tied" to the stone. Which seems to indicate that these two moments in the year were of particular spiritual or ritual significance to the Incas.

In more modern history, harvest festivals have become closely linked to the Autumn Equinox. Agricultural communities would hold harvest festivals at the end of the growing season, to give thanks for the safe gathering of the crops and to celebrate with feasts and song. Apple harvests in particular traditionally take place in September and October, and in many cultures, the apple is seen as a sacred or magical fruit, so apples have become a powerful magical symbol associated with the Autumn Equinox. Rituals connected to harvest festivals follow themes of abundance and gratitude, and they are traditionally held on the full moon that falls closest to the Autumn Equinox (known as the Harvest Moon). Many modern Autumn Equinox celebrations continue this theme of gratitude and thanksgiving.

# Sun God of the Season

## RA

Ra was an Ancient Egyptian sun god and he is often portrayed as a human with the head of a falcon topped with a golden sun disc. In Egyptian mythology Ra travelled across the sky every day bringing light and warmth to the earth below, but rather than travelling in a chariot, as is common in sun god mythology, he did so in a sky boat. At sunset, he had to travel into the underworld to battle the demons of that realm, including the serpent Apophis who was intent on destroying the sun and, with it, all life on earth. Each morning Ra would emerge from the underworld victorious, bringing the dawn once again to the people of the earth. If a solar eclipse occurred, it was thought that Apophis had finally managed to catch Ra, if only for a moment.

# 10 Modern Rituals to Welcome the Autumn

At a time when the landscape around us is golden and ripe, equinox celebrations focus on thanksgiving, harvest, and abundance. From preserving and bottling the harvest, to bringing autumn colours into our homes, and feasting with friends and family, the Autumn Equinox is a time for us to gather together to give thanks for the summer.

Whether you take a walk in the woods to soak up all the glorious colours, or get busy bottling and preserving harvest produce, there is plenty to do and enjoy at the equinox. It's also a time to be still, for just a moment, and to acknowledge the gentle shift of solar energy, and to welcome and savour the start of a slower, gentler season. Here are a few ways to bring the rich warmth of the autumn sun into your equinox celebrations.

THE AUTUMN EQUINOX IS A TIME TO GATHER TOGETHER TO GIVE THANKS FOR THE SUMMER

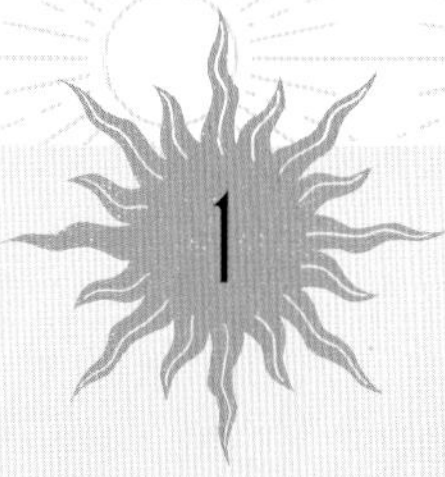


# WATCH A SUNRISE OR SUNSET

The simplest and gentlest way to celebrate any solar festival is to greet the sun as it rises on equinox morning. We will be greeting the dawn on each of the solar festival days throughout the year, giving us a chance to stop and notice all the changes around us.

There may be a gathering place near you where you can meet with others to watch the sunrise; Stonehenge in the UK usually attracts visitors on the Autumn Equinox, as do a handful of other ancient monuments around the world. Or you could mark this point of balance and alignment by greeting the dawn in your own way by rising early, and quietly watching the sun rise from your own home.

The Autumn Equinox marks the start of diminishing light. From this point on, each day will become gradually shorter as we head towards the shortest day of the year at the Winter Solstice. But now is the moment to offer gratitude for the summer season, as well as offering up your hopes and wishes for the new season ahead.

You could watch the sunset on this day, too, as at the equinox, sunrise and sunset will be almost exactly 12 hours apart, which feels particularly special.

# MAKE A GRATITUDE LIST

In contrast to the Spring Equinox, which is fully focused on rising energy levels and looking forward to summer, the Autumn Equinox is a time to look back at the year and reflect on it, to give thanks for the summer and to gather in the harvest, both literally and metaphorically. Thanksgiving for a successful summer and harvest is the main theme at this time of year, but this doesn't just mean a literal harvest, it can relate to anything in your life. Friendships, hobbies, family, work; now is the time to acknowledge whatever it is that you feel grateful about and are thankful for.

Take a moment on the equinox, or in the days surrounding it, to take a piece of paper and write out everything you are grateful for. If you're not sure where to start, begin with the basics: your home, your surroundings, your community. Then add the people in your life you are grateful for, experiences you've had this year, places you've seen, food you've enjoyed, work that felt meaningful. Anything and everything that pops into your head. Keep the list somewhere safe, so you can look at it anytime you might need to. This could also be a good activity to do with friends and family at an Autumn Equinox meal or gathering.

# BOTTLE THE SUN

Many of the foods we harvest in autumn are bursting with the warmth and light of summer, from ripe orange pumpkins to sweet pears and crisp apples. Harvest season gives us an opportunity to take some of this golden summer sun into the autumn and winter by carefully preserving and storing as much of it as possible. As we work hard to preserve any vegetable or fruit gluts at the equinox, we are essentially bottling the sun and taking it with us into the dark half of the year. Think of it as a talisman to ensure the sun's safe return.

Here are a couple of ways you can preserve an Autumn Equinox harvest and take it into the winter with you.

## STORE APPLES

Apples will keep for a long time if they are carefully picked and stored, and your equinox harvest could last you right through the winter, if you're lucky. To store apples correctly, you must:

**1.** Pick your apples carefully and handle them gently to avoid bruising. Keep the stem intact, if possible.

**2.** Check the apples for any cuts, holes, or blemishes, and discard any with these.

**3.** Wrap each apple in a sheet of newspaper and place them individually on a wooden shelf or in a wooden crate, ensuring no apples touch each other.

**4.** Place them somewhere cool and dark (but not where they can experience frost) like a shed or garage.

**5.** Check them now and again to make sure none have started to rot, as one rotten apple could ruin the whole lot if allowed to spread.

**6.** Enjoy them right through winter.

## FREEZE A BLACKBERRY HARVEST

Sun-ripened and sweet, with just a hint of something darker and smokier underneath; there's no better bridge between summer and autumn than a blackberry. They manage to combine all the happiness and sunshine of summer with the richness of autumn, in a deeply comforting way. Here's how to preserve a late summer/early autumn berry harvest to be enjoyed all through winter:

**1.** Wash your blackberries thoroughly with cold water and remove any debris, leaves, and stems.

**2.** Gently pat them dry, then allow them to completely air dry on a kitchen towel.

**3.** Once dry, place them on a baking sheet, ensuring none of the berries are touching.

**4.** Place the baking sheet in the freezer and "flash freeze" them for a few hours. This ensures they freeze individually rather than sticking together.

**5.** Once frozen, remove the tray from the freezer and scoop the berries into a freezer bag or container.

**6.** Store them in the freezer so you can enjoy them throughout autumn and winter.

**7.** The berries should last for about 6–9 months in the freezer – giving you the chance to enjoy summer-ripe fruit right through until the Spring Equinox, or even the Summer Solstice.

**8.** Frozen berries can be used throughout the winter to make cobblers and pies, or can be added to breakfast cereal or pancake batter. They can even be made into blackberry jam.

# SAVE SEEDS AND PLANT BULBS

Although the summer growing season is over, now is the perfect time to plant flower bulbs for next spring. So if you like the idea of picking your own flowers at the Spring Equinox, you need to get the bulbs into the ground now. Narcissi, crocus, and muscari bulbs are perfect to plant at this time of year, as they're simple to dig in and need minimal care between now and spring, when they will reward you with the brightest of flowers around the time of the equinox.

Now is also the time to save seeds from your summer flowers and vegetables for planting again in the spring. If you grew sunflowers this summer, harvesting the seeds will provide you with a huge bounty of seeds for next year. If you grew beans, squashes, or pumpkins this year, make sure to dry and save some of the seeds for next year, too. Place dry seeds in paper envelopes, clearly label and date them, and place them somewhere cool and dry. Seeds also make an excellent Autumn Equinox gift.

## START A NEW CRAFT OR HOBBY

Many people notice a new sense of energy and purpose in autumn. I seem to get a burst of creative energy at this time of year, probably linked to the cooling weather and the lengthening evenings, which are suited to more indoor-based activities. There's just something about being on the threshold of a new season that brings a sense of renewal and fresh energy. In fact some believe that previous cultures saw autumn as the start of their calendar (rather than starting in January as we do today). If you also feel a new sense of energy and creativity at this time of year, now is a good time to channel that energy into a new craft or hobby. Preferably a cosy indoor one that can keep you occupied and happy as the days shorten and the evenings lengthen.

Journaling or creative writing are great to try at this time of year; the quieter, more reflective energy that comes with the shortening days can help you to tap into your intuition and allow it to flow freely. Tactile crafts that engage your senses, such as knitting or crochet, can also come into their own in autumn, offering a cosy and more creative alternative to scrolling on a phone or device as the evenings lengthen.

# LOOK FOR BALANCE

This brief moment of solar balance is the perfect time to take stock of what is in balance in your life and what might need adjusting. Modern equinox celebrations tend to focus on rituals like this to help settle and reset before launching into a new season. Below is my take on a rebalancing ritual that can be repeated at each of the equinoxes.

This should be a gentle ritual that makes you feel optimistic, so don't worry about it or put any pressure on yourself, just know that by checking in at each equinox, you're taking gentle steps to achieve balance and happiness. Just relax, write intuitively and enjoy the process. Light a candle, make a warm drink, and settle in.

## AUTUMN EQUINOX "REBALANCING" RITUAL

### YOU WILL NEED

- 2 pieces of A4 (letter) paper
- Pen
- Scissors
- Magazines, catalogues, or other visual materials for mood boarding
- Glue stick

### METHOD

**1.** On your first piece of paper write a list of all the things you'd like to invite more into your life. Think about what you would spend more time doing in an ideal world. Things that would help you to feel more balanced. Whatever springs to mind, write it down. Don't think too much about how you're going to achieve these things; just fill your page with lovely ideas.

**2.** Now it's time to add images to this list of words. I'm a visual person, so I love an excuse to get creative, but if this doesn't appeal to you, then it's not essential. I do find, however, that it can often be easier to identify what it is that we long for when we collect visual materials. A common thread or recurring theme often presents itself to you completely unbidden. Not sure what you want, but keep collecting images on a particular theme? Let the images lead you. It's nice to go analogue for this too, cutting and sticking real pictures with real scissors and glue. Give your eyes and shoulders a digital-screen break.

**3.** When you've finished this, take your beautifully decorated list and place it somewhere you can see it every day. This bit is important. You want to focus your attention on this list of lovely things that feel important and deeply personal to you. So put it somewhere you can see it easily every day.

**4.** Now, on the second piece of paper, write down anything that you feel takes up too much time in your life or that you would like to let go of. Again, don't overthink this; just follow your intuition. This list doesn't get the mood board treatment, though! We don't want to focus any creative energy on things we want to reduce or get rid of. So just write a simple list.

**5.** Tuck this second list away somewhere out of sight, but keep it safe and we'll check in with it again at the Spring Equinox.

That's it. Now there's nothing more to do, or worry about. By acknowledging all the things you want to invite more of, you're taking gentle steps towards bringing them into your life. And by writing down things you want to let go of, you've already taken the first step towards releasing them.

We'll check in again with both our lists at the Spring Equinox and with any luck they will have started to gently pull a little bit more into balance without you even realizing.

# BAKE CINNAMON-SCENTED TREATS

From apple pies and crumbles to pumpkin-spiced drinks, Autumn Equinox baking is all about rich, nostalgic flavours that make the most of the year's harvest. Aromatic spices like cinnamon and ginger make a strong appearance at this time of year, too. Below is a recipe for cinnamon-glazed autumn leaf cookies; they are quick to make and will fill your house with autumn warmth as they bake in the oven.

## AUTUMN LEAF COOKIES

These cinnamon and ginger cookies are warming and sweet and would go perfectly with a pumpkin-spiced latte. You can make them any shape you like; leaf-shaped cookie cutters work well, but so do pumpkins, apples, mushrooms, and bats. Choose whatever feels autumnal to you!

### INGREDIENTS

- 300g (10oz) plain (all-purpose) flour, plus extra for dusting
- 1 tsp ground ginger
- 1 tsp ground cinnamon, plus extra to decorate
- 1 tsp bicarbonate of soda (baking soda)
- 100g (3½oz) softened butter
- 100g (3½oz) caster (superfine) sugar
- 1 egg
- 3 tbsp golden syrup (or corn syrup)
- 100g (3½oz) icing (confectioners') sugar, to decorate

**METHOD**

**1.** Preheat the oven to 190°C/175°C fan/Gas 5 (375°F). Line a baking sheet with baking (parchment) paper.

**2.** Sift the flour, spices, and bicarbonate of soda together into a mixing bowl.

**3.** Add the butter and rub it into the flour by hand to until it has a breadcrumb texture.

**4.** Stir in the sugar.

**5.** Add the egg and golden syrup and mix everything together to make a smooth dough.

**6.** Lightly flour your work surface and rolling pin.

**7.** Roll out the dough to a thickness of 5mm (¼in).

**8.** Cut out leaf shapes using the cutters and place them on the lined baking sheet.

**9.** Bake for 10–12 minutes until they are a very light golden colour.

**10.** Cool on a wire rack.

**11.** To ice (frost) the cookies, add a small pinch of ground cinnamon to the icing sugar, then add just enough water to make a smooth (frosting) icing and use to decorate your cookies.

Once they are done, these cookies will keep fresh for 3 days in an airtight tin.

# HOLD A HARVEST MEAL

Harvest festivals are inextricably linked with the Autumn Equinox and harvest meals, and celebrations are usually held on the closest weekend to the Harvest Moon. This is the full moon that falls closest to the Autumn Equinox, either in late September or early October. If you fancy hosting your own harvest meal, here are a few key elements to consider:

- Celebrate seasonal food and drink. The key to a good harvest supper is to choose hearty, warming food that's linked to the season. Apple cakes and crumbles are a delicious traditional dessert to cook at this time of year, and a great way to celebrate local produce.
- Keep it casual and social. Ask everyone to bring what they can to create a pot-luck dinner, and keep the focus on the company rather than worrying about a fancy meal. That said, you do need someone organized in charge of planning this bit so you don't end up with four apple crumbles and no main course.
- Eat outdoors if the weather permits.
- Decorate your table with autumnal foliage and flowers. Rustic is the name of the game here, so jugs of flowers, branches of foliage, and berries are ideal, as are tealights in jam jars. See Autumn Equinox Crafts to make your own autumn leaf lantern.

- Plan some sort of harvest-based entertainment. This doesn't have to be anything too adventurous; a harvest-themed music playlist would be an excellent idea. You could also try some outdoor games after dinner.
- Make a harvest donation box and ask everyone to bring a tin, jar, or packet of food, if they can spare one. You can then take it to a food bank or charity afterwards to pass on the abundance of this time of year.

**WHAT TO INCLUDE IN YOUR HARVEST MEAL**

- Butternut squash soup
- Slow-cooked stews and casseroles
- Roasted root vegetables
- Freshly baked bread in the shape of a wheatsheaf or sun
- Apple crumble
- Blackberry cobbler
- Pumpkin pie
- Apple cider

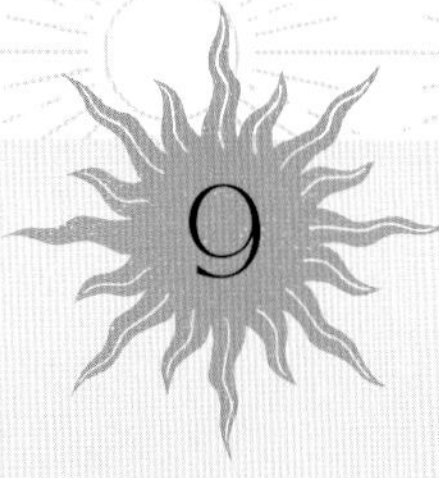

# TAKE AN AUTUMN COLOUR WALK

Walking in the woods is obligatory this month. The colours of the leaves, the abundance of berries and nuts, the mushroomy, earthy smell, the crunchiness underfoot; there is so much to see outdoors. This is the time to enjoy the outdoors in that lovely early autumn stage, while everything is gently starting to shift and turn but the weather is still mild enough to head out without bundling up in too many layers.

## WHAT YOU MIGHT SPOT

If you're lucky and you pick one of those beautiful early autumn days where a soft morning mist burns off to reveal golden sunshine, it doesn't get much better than that. You might spot dew-soaked spiderwebs, leaves that are just starting to turn, mushrooms, nuts, and berries. September skies can be some of the most beautiful of the entire year; there's a particular kind of deep, clear blue that is unique to this month. Combined with the strong, rich colours of the trees and hedgerows, September can be a beautiful month to be outside.

In the garden there is still plenty to enjoy as flowers shift into rich, autumnal colours, with some continuing to flower right up until the first frost. The first berries and hips are starting to cover the hedgerows, too, adding rich colour and, of course, the trees hit their beautiful best in the weeks around the equinox as the first leaves start to change into their autumn golds, yellows, and reds. You will also start to see tree seeds, like acorns, conkers (horse chestnuts), and beech mast, scattered under the trees.

Autumn is also mushroom season, and if you're really lucky, you might spot a fairy ring. This is a perfect circle of mushrooms that can appear sometimes overnight, on a lawn or forest floor, said to be a portal into the fairy realm. If you do see one, treat it with respect and caution, as many folktales have been told about those who step into a fairy ring never to return.

As for wildlife, autumn is a busy season, as many animals prepare for the cold season by stocking up on autumn berries and nuts. Deer begin their dramatic rutting season in the autumn, and you might also see large flocks of birds massing and preparing to migrate to warmer shores. You could also hear the distinctive call of an owl if you're out at dusk, as autumn is when some owl species start to defend their territories and look for a mate, giving equinox evenings an eerie and magical atmosphere.

# UPDATE YOUR SEASONAL SHELF

A simple and lovely way to connect yourself to the changing seasons is to create a seasonal shelf or display area in your home that you update throughout the year. Whether you want to call this a display shelf, a seasonal collection, or a nature altar is completely up to you, but it's nice to have a focal point indoors to reflect the seasons. You can fill your shelf with anything that signals the changing seasons to you.

I like to bring in a few pieces of treasure from outside such as flowers, grasses, or leaves: anything I've picked up on my walks or in the garden. Alongside this I will add a candle and a solar symbol. I might also add a photo that sums up the spirit of this time of year for me, or display one or two of my favourite seasonal books. I don't overthink it too much and I don't "style" it; this is just for me, so I instinctively collect things throughout the year to add to it, and I change it to reflect the solar seasons. The beauty of a seasonal shelf or altar is that no two will be the same; yours will be completely bespoke and personal to you and you should fill it with things that bring you joy.

At this time of year it's all about early autumn treasures. You might like to bring in acorns, conkers, leaves, and rosehips to display this month. You could also display your favourite cosy autumnal books.

Children might also like to start their own seasonal shelf and it can be useful to have a dedicated space to collect all the tiny treasures they inevitably return home with after a day spent outside. You can use this shelf as a way to gently signal all the seasonal changes throughout the year. You can also rotate a selection of seasonal story books and activity books on this table.

If you need some ideas to get started with your own seasonal shelf or nature table for the Autumn Equinox, you might like to bring in some of the following items:

- A dish of acorns or conkers.
- A vase of autumn flowers, foliage, or berries.
- Apples or other seasonal fruit.
- Seasonal books that represent the Autumn Equinox or the harvest season.
- A decoration, drawing, or ornament that represents the sun.
- A candle in gold, yellow, or orange.

# Autumn Equinox Crafts

## AUTUMN LEAF LANTERN

Keep the sun shining as the days start to shorten with this golden autumn leaf lantern. It couldn't be easier to make, and it will cast a cheerful light on an autumn night. You'll need to press your leaves first to preserve them, but if you do this in advance, the lantern itself takes only a short while to make and is a very therapeutic craft for an autumn evening.

**YOU WILL NEED**

- Autumn leaves
- Absorbent paper, for pressing
- Flower press or heavy books
- Glass jar
- Clear-drying craft glue (like PVA)
- Paintbrush
- Tealight (candle or battery powered)

**HERE'S HOW TO MAKE YOUR OWN AUTUMN LEAF LANTERN**

**1.** Take your autumn leaves and press them flat between two pieces of absorbent paper. Place them in a flower press or under a few heavy books for a couple of weeks until they are pressed and dry. Ensure they are stored somewhere warm and dry to speed up the process.

**2.** Take your clean glass jar and apply a thin layer of craft glue around the outside of the jar with the paintbrush.

**3.** Add your pressed leaves to create any pattern you like. I like to cover as much of the glass as possible to create a stained-glass effect for the light to shine through. You can overlap the leaves.

**4.** When you've finished, apply a thin layer of glue over the top of the leaves.

**5.** Allow to dry completely.

**6.** Add your tealight, light it carefully, then step back and admire.

# GOLDEN LEAF GARLAND

One way to preserve the golden colours of the sun for a little bit longer is to create a leaf garland to decorate your home. Dipping leaves in natural beeswax helps to preserve them for longer and gives them a beautifully warm scent of honey.

**YOU WILL NEED**

- Autumn leaves
- Saucepan
- Heatproof glass bowl
- Beeswax pellets, for melting
- Pegs or paperclips
- String or gold thread

**HERE'S HOW TO MAKE YOUR OWN GOLDEN LEAF GARLAND**

**1.** Collect a range of different shaped autumn leaves in as many different shades of yellow, orange, and red as you can find. Larger leaves are best, but small ones can work too.

**2.** Fill a saucepan with water, then place the heatproof bowl into the saucepan so it floats in the water. Add the beeswax pellets to the bowl and gently heat the water until the wax melts to a liquid.

**3.** Remove the saucepan from the heat, but keep the bowl sitting in the hot water, to keep the wax molten.

**4.** Holding each leaf by the stem, dip them in the wax one by one, thinly coating each side. This will help to preserve their colour.

**5.** Peg or paperclip the wax-dipped leaves to a length of string and allow them to completely air-dry. Smaller leaves work best with pegs, or you can glue them to the string. The beeswax might dry slightly yellow rather than clear, but this doesn't matter at all – it adds to the golden effect.

**6.** Once dry, tie your leaves by the stems onto a length of string or gold thread at regular intervals to create an autumn leaf garland bursting with sunshine colours.

**7.** String up at a window or across a bookshelf or mantelpiece for everyone to enjoy.

# HARVEST SAUCER

A harvest saucer is a bit like a nature mandala: a circular pattern made up of natural materials found outside in the autumn. The circular sun shape of the saucer and the warm shades of yellow, orange, and red used within it are a fitting tribute to the golden sun that has made the harvest possible. This equinox activity is one I used to look forward to every year as a child; we made them at school to decorate our local church for the harvest season. It's a really simple thing to make, and can be very soothing and meditative: a great activity for children or adults alike.

**YOU WILL NEED**

- Clean saucer or small circular plate
- Small amount of wet sand
- Autumn leaves, nuts, seeds, berries, or other autumn treasures

**HERE'S HOW TO MAKE YOUR OWN HARVEST SAUCER**

**1.** Fill your saucer or plate with sand and smooth it across to level out the top.

**2.** Decorate the saucer with your autumn treasure to create a pattern that radiates out from the centre. You can use leaves, nuts, berries, flowers, beautiful stones – anything you can find outside at this time of year.

**3.** The finished result can be as neat or as wild as you like – this is where your creativity comes into its own.

**4.** If the sand is regularly sprayed with water to keep it damp, this decoration will last for a good few days.

**5.** Use yours as a table centrepiece or place it in a window.

# AUTUMN SEEDCAKES (FOR THE BIRDS)

As the cooler weather approaches, now is the time to look after your local wildlife. Making pinecone seedcakes for the birds is calming and fun, and a great activity to get children involved with too. This particular craft uses only natural materials, so it's a safe, biodegradable decoration to leave outdoors.

**YOU WILL NEED**

- String
- Pinecones
- Lard or vegetable fat, at room temperature
- Bird seed

**HERE'S HOW TO MAKE YOUR OWN AUTUMN SEED CAKES**

**1.** Tie a piece of string to the top of your pinecones.

**2.** Put the lard or vegetable fat in a bowl and mix in the bird seed to make a paste.

**3.** Press the seed mix carefully into all the gaps in the pinecones.

**4.** Hang on a tree in the garden.

# Winter Solstice

# What is the Winter Solstice?

The Winter Solstice occurs when the Earth is at its maximum tilt away from the Sun, creating the longest night and the shortest day of the year.

In the Northern Hemisphere this typically falls between 20 and 23 December and it marks the official start of astronomical winter. However some believe the solstice actually marks the midpoint of the season, hence the name "Midwinter", which is also used to describe this time of year.

After this day the balance will start to shift towards the light again, and the amount of sunlight each day will increase slowly but surely as we turn towards the Spring Equinox.

# How Does it Affect Us?

In the ebb and flow of the year, winter is a beautiful season of deep rest. As daylight levels fade, so too do many of the pressures, jobs, and activities of the previous season, and with the dark half of the year comes the permission to do a lot *less*. Which is exactly what we should be doing, because at the time of the Winter Solstice the hours of sunlight are at their shortest, and the effect of the short days on our bodies and minds can be profound.

At the darkest point in the year, we have a much smaller window of opportunity in which to absorb sunlight each day, so we have less opportunity to soak up all that solar energy or to produce the vitamin D that is our bodies' vital response to it. We might also experience lower energy levels or feel the need to sleep more during the long, dark nights. This change can be felt most keenly in the most northerly countries where the sun barely rises at this time of year, a time of almost perpetual night. Now is the time to be very kind to ourselves.

As the natural world around us stills and starts to feed its energy into the earth, this is the moment for peace and reflection. As we reach the darkest point of the year at the Winter Solstice this is a time to listen to, and take care of, our bodies; to rest and not put too much strain on ourselves. The natural world is in a phase of deep sleep right now. As trees and plants reach their roots down into the dark quiet of the earth, and animals retreat into their dens, this is the time for us to cosy down into our homes too and take the opportunity to replenish after a busy year.

If you walk outside in nature at the Winter Solstice it can feel like there is a heavy layer of peace gently covering everything, and ideally we should afford ourselves the same level of stillness and rest at this time of year. That can be easier said than done though; often the winter months can be a time of intense activity and busyness for many of us. We've become used to fighting the dark evenings with bright artificial lights, rushing our way through the season, and pushing ourselves with busy schedules and festive activities. It's no wonder many of us feel exhausted by the end of December and hollow in January; our bodies just aren't designed to work that hard during the dark winter months.

If we can find a way to take our cues from the natural world, though, and instead embrace the dark evenings and use them as a time to rest, heal, and reflect on the passing year, we might find ourselves approaching the season with a renewed appreciation for the gifts it can offer. This is not a time to overexert ourselves; it's a time for sinking into the comfort of our homes, reflecting on the year past, connecting with our ancestors and telling stories around a fire as the nights tick gently by. Above all it's a time for conserving our energy and being kind to ourselves. The days are short, but that means evenings are long and peaceful. There are warming fires to look forward to, books to read, candles to light and, above all, stories to tell. Because this is a season of storytelling. The dark nights are made for it and the folklore of winter is pleasingly rich; filled with wolves, owls, and ancient spirits that come to life around a crackling fire.

And then, of course, winter gives us a real gift, right at the darkest moment, with the Winter Solstice festival. Winter Solstice celebrations are ancient and have followed a simple, nature-based pattern for centuries; for a few days in December we cast off the cosy blanket of hibernation and sprinkle a little magic and sunlight across this time of deep Midwinter. Candles and hearth fires are lit, family and friends join together, evergreens and winter berries are gathered and brought indoors, and we remind ourselves, on the darkest night, that the sun will return. As we kindle the sun back into life, through light, warmth, and friendship, we take time to give thanks for it and reassure ourselves that from this day onwards, we are slowly but steadily walking back towards the light.

And after all that solstice celebration and feasting, you have my full permission to return under the cloak of hibernation for another few weeks, until the Spring Equinox calls us out again into the light. Because although the longest night has passed, we are still in the thick of winter, and now is not the time for rushing anything. Life will pick up pace soon enough, so make the most of this long, lovely season of rest while you can and follow the lead of our pagan ancestors, continuing the hibernation season well into January and focusing on all the slow, gentle, and cosy aspects of this season.

THIS IS NOT A TIME TO OVEREXERT OURSELVES; IT'S A TIME FOR SINKING INTO THE COMFORT OF OUR HOMES, REFLECTING ON THE YEAR PAST, CONNECTING WITH OUR ANCESTORS AND TELLING STORIES AROUND A FIRE AS THE NIGHTS TICK GENTLY BY

# Ancient Magic and Folklore of the Winter Solstice

Of all the festivals in the solar year, the Winter Solstice is one of the most ancient and universally celebrated, woven through with rituals, traditions, and stories from across countries and cultures. Because the sun appears to "stand still" in the sky for a few days around the solstice, the longest night has long been a time for dreaming, for magic, and for incantations to bring the sun safely back for another year.

Celebrating the return of the light is never more important than on the darkest day of the year, and one thing all cultures have in common when celebrating the Winter Solstice is the ritual worship of the sun. From Ancient Roman celebrations of Saturnalia, to Norse Yule fires, and candlelight carol services, it has long been traditional to fill this dark month with fire and light. Ancient monuments to sun worship at the solstice, such as Stonehenge, can be found sprinkled across the world, and people still flock to them today to watch the sun rise on solstice morning.

The Midwinter festival has also traditionally been a deeply nature-based celebration day. From the evergreen branches used to dress Roman temples and homes, and the mistletoe and holly favoured by the ancient Celts, many of these natural elements still form the basis of our winter celebrations today in the Northern Hemisphere.

Then, of course, there is the element of magic and mystery that is woven through our solstice celebrations. The nights around Midwinter have long been linked with otherworldly happenings. In contrast to Summer Solstice folktales and myths, which are concerned with mischief and mayhem, the Winter Solstice folktales are a gentler kind, filled with kind deeds, wishes granted, and gifts delivered in secret.

Above all, at a time of year when the days are short and the sun seems far away, solstice celebrations are overwhelmingly warm, inclusive, and joyful, as if we are all determined to bring the warmth and brightness of the sun back to life at a time when it is needed most.

# Sun God of the Season

## SOL

Sol was an Ancient Roman sun god who was often depicted with a crown of sun rays or driving a chariot drawn by four horses.

In the late Roman period, Sol was celebrated as *Sol Invictus*, which means "unconquered sun", and celebrations were thought to have been held in his honour each year on 25 December (the date of the Winter Solstice in the old Julian calendar). This day may have been known as *Dies Natalis Solis Invicti* or the "Birthday of the Invincible Sun". This date also marked the end of the Ancient Roman festival of Saturnalia, a period of several days of Midwinter feasting, gift-giving, and celebration, which many believe was the blueprint for our modern-day winter festivities.

Like most sun gods, Sol Invictus was seen as a powerful emblem of strength, as he rose each day to banish the darkness and bring light. Worshipping him on the darkest day of the year was a clear call for the rebirth of the sun.

# 10 Modern Rituals to Welcome the Winter

At a time when the days are short and the landscape is dark and quiet, solstice celebrations focus on the rebirth of the sun and the return of the light. Many different cultures have observed the Winter Solstice, and over time elements of these ancient festivals have merged with newer traditions to become the festive season as we know it today.

It's interesting to see how many of the traditions we celebrate actually have their roots in these early pagan traditions of sun and nature worship, from decorating our homes with evergreens and winter berries to lighting the darkness with candles and warm fires.

The solstice, or Midwinter, is a time to gather together, give thanks for the past year, and look towards brighter days.

Here are a few ways to bring the spirit of the Winter Solstice into your festive celebrations.

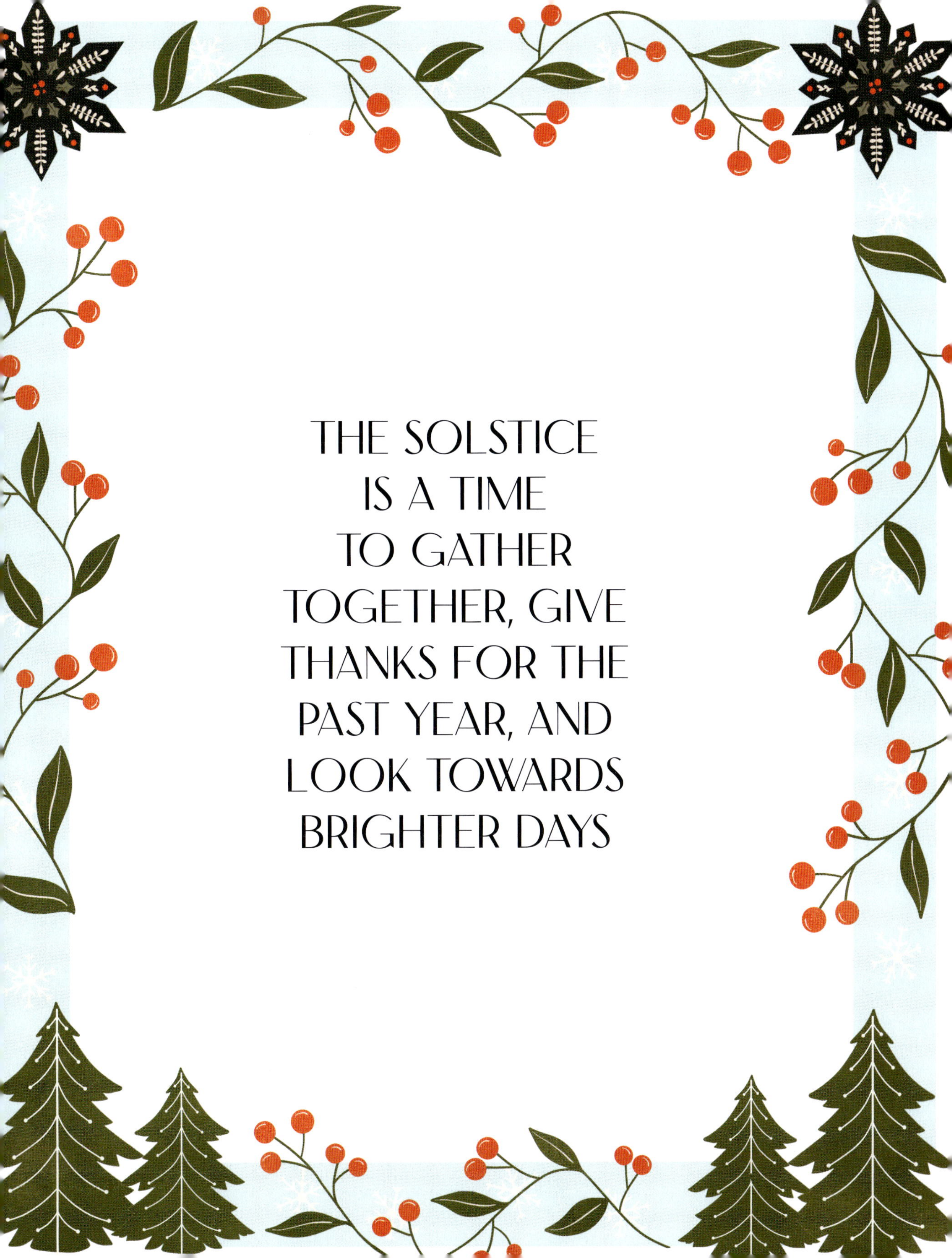
THE SOLSTICE
IS A TIME
TO GATHER
TOGETHER, GIVE
THANKS FOR THE
PAST YEAR, AND
LOOK TOWARDS
BRIGHTER DAYS

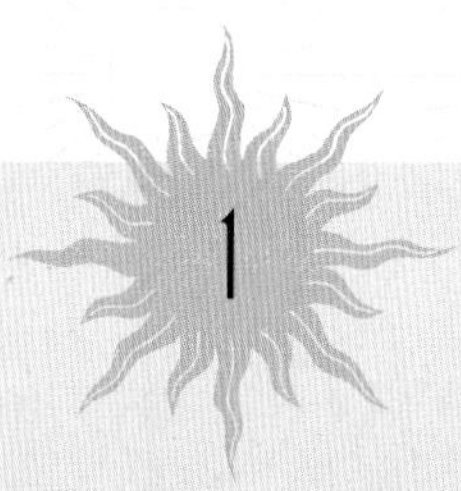

# GREET THE DAWN

As with all the solar festivals in the book, we're going to start the day by greeting the sun as it rises at dawn. The good news is that at this time of year, sunrise is the latest it will be all year, so you won't need to get up especially early to do this.

Some people choose to gather at sacred places of ancient sun worship on the morning of the solstice, to witness and celebrate the sunrise with others. The standing stones of Stonehenge are one of the most instantly recognisable of these ancient monuments, and each year at the solstice the stones are opened up for visitors to gather and experience the sunrise communally.

Wherever you choose to watch the sunrise, at this dark, magical time of year it feels particularly special to be able to experience sunrise in exactly the same way as our ancestors did all those years ago. You can almost feel their relief and jubilation at the thought that the darkest moment has passed and that from this morning onwards, the sun will grow stronger and stronger each day.

And if you miss the sunrise? Don't worry; there's always sunset. Although these days people gather at Stonehenge to watch the sunrise, It's believed the stones were actually originally structured to frame the Midwinter *sunset* during the Winter Solstice. So if you miss the dawn, instead keep an eye out for the sunset, and give the sun a gentle nod of thanks as it sets on the shortest day of the year.

# LIGHT A YULE LOG

Continue a Midwinter ritual started by the Vikings and bring in a ceremonial Yule log to light during the Midwinter festivities. The Yule log is a winter ritual from the Scandinavian tradition, where a log, usually from an oak tree, was burned for the duration of the Yule celebrations to encourage the sun to return. This log would supposedly be used to keep the fire going for the 12 days of the Yule festival, and a small piece of the log would then be kept to kindle next year's fire.

It's interesting that at both the darkest and lightest points of the year, fires are a key part of the ceremonies around each day. At the Summer Solstice fires are lit to strengthen and celebrate the full power of the sun on the longest day, whereas at the Winter Solstice they are lit as a symbol of the sun's returning power and strength, to remind us that brighter, warmer days will return.

If you're able to light a fire at home or outside, you could choose your own ceremonial Yule log and invite friends and family to help you ceremonially light the first fire of the festival. As the flames catch and the fire breathes into life, take a moment to offer thanks for the year that has passed, and to celebrate the return of the sun from this day onwards. Don't forget to save a piece of the Yule log to light next year's fire.

# SPEND A DAY BY CANDLELIGHT

Another way to fill your home with light at the Winter Solstice is to light candles, and plenty of them. A tiny but powerful emblem of returning light, candles can cast a glittering layer of warmth across solstice celebrations. When used instead of electric light to illuminate the early winter evenings or dark, quiet mornings, they can make this time of year feel magical. On the longest, darkest night of the year, it's traditional to light a candle at sunset, then leave some kind of (safe) light burning overnight until the sun rises on solstice dawn. But you can fill the days and weeks surrounding the solstice with candlelight too; we are in the depths of Midwinter and light is needed more than ever.

Natural wax candles such as beeswax are the best option for a sustainable source of candlelight. Candles scented with essential oils such as orange or frankincense can also bring a layer of spiced winter warmth to the season. Dot them liberally around your home, use them to light the table at mealtimes, and place them (safely) in windows for passers-by to enjoy.

Safety Note: always place candles on fire-proof, stable bases or in candle holders, away from flammable materials such as paper or curtains (drapes). Never leave a burning candle unattended.

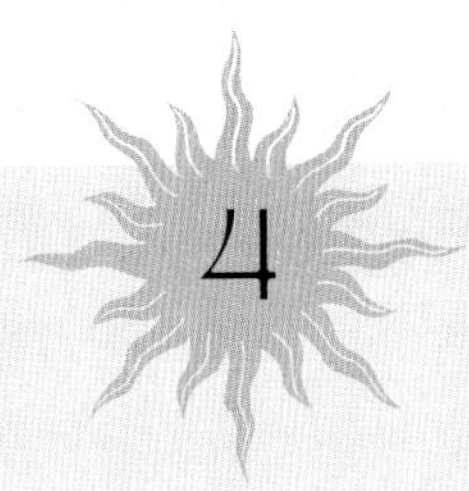

## EMBRACE HIBERNATION RITUALS

If you've wanted to embrace the slow living movement, now is your moment. No other season lends itself to this way of living more than gentle, sleepy winter, so if you feel the need to settle down early in the evenings, don't fight it. In direct contrast to the Summer Solstice where we are more likely to feel extroverted and sociable, the Winter Solstice is a time for drawing down into ourselves, pulling our energy inwards, and spending time with our thoughts and inner life.

December can be a deeply peaceful month if you want it to be. If you look to nature for clues, the time around the solstice is all about hunkering down, shedding unnecessary layers, and settling into the dark season. Now is a time for reading, dreaming, writing, sketching: whatever it is that refreshes your soul and feeds your inner life. Often the real magic of the season lies in these quiet, still moments throughout December where we allow our minds to drift and dream. If your book pile didn't get a look in over the summer months, now is the time to lose yourself in the pages of a novel, or to pick up a soothing craft project that allows your mind to wander while you stitch or draw.

In this cold, dark month it also pays to follow the advice of the Danes who are well used to finding happiness in the winter thanks to their now-famous concept of "hygge". The word *hygge* is thought to derive from the Old Norse word meaning "protected from the outside world", which seems very appropriate for this month. So whatever helps you to do that is to be encouraged. Lighting candles, wearing only cosy clothes, saying no to going out; whatever you choose, just call it *hygge* and it will immediately change from "slightly lazy" to "wholesome and Scandinavian". The sun will soon return, too, so make the most of the quiet solar energy around this time of year while you can and sink into relaxation and rest.

# BRING IN EVERGREENS

"Bringing the outside in" gets literal in December when, for a few weeks, it is totally normal and acceptable to drag an entire tree indoors and stand it in the corner of your living room. Historically this tree would have been covered with tiny candles, shining a light into the dark, although these days we are more likely to cover them with tiny twinkling electric lights.

Although the indoor Christmas tree was popularized by the Victorians, people have been decorating their homes with evergreen branches for centuries. As plants that kept their colour in the winter, evergreens were celebrated as a symbol of everlasting life and regeneration in the depths of winter. They've been linked to solstice celebrations since ancient Roman times when evergreen branches and wreaths were used to decorate temples and homes for the Midwinter Roman festival of Saturnalia. Bringing branches of evergreens indoors also brings in a wonderfully spicy, earthy scent that can help to link us to the outside at a time when doors and windows are usually kept firmly closed. It's a uniquely Midwinter smell that's both comforting and nostalgic.

Holly and mistletoe are two other evergreen plants that have become synonymous with modern day Christmas celebrations, but they were important in pre-Christian celebrations too. As some of the few plants that retain their colour and provide berries through winter, they were regarded by ancient civilizations as potent symbols of regeneration and life. Holly trees are deeply connected to solstice celebrations, and in folklore they are widely considered to have magical and sacred properties. According to ancient lore, it's considered bad luck to cut down a holly tree. However conversely, taking branches and cuttings from a holly tree are considered to be good luck charms when brought into the home, provided you ask permission from the tree first, and make sure to leave an offering afterwards. Which seems a sensible approach when taking anything from nature.

Mistletoe has also been used as a symbol of Midwinter regeneration since pre-Christian times. Mistletoe grows on oak trees, which were regarded as sacred in pagan culture, and because it produces fruit at this time of year mistletoe was traditionally cut and used as decoration at the time of the solstice. (Do take care when bringing mistletoe indoors though, as the berries are toxic, so should be kept away from children and animals.)

And if you really want to do things correctly, according to ancient Celtic tradition, mistletoe should be harvested on the sixth day of the moon, and it should be cut from the tree with a golden sickle and then caught before it touches the ground to ensure its magical powers remain intact. If golden sickles are hard to come by, though, you could always try your local market for mistletoe instead.

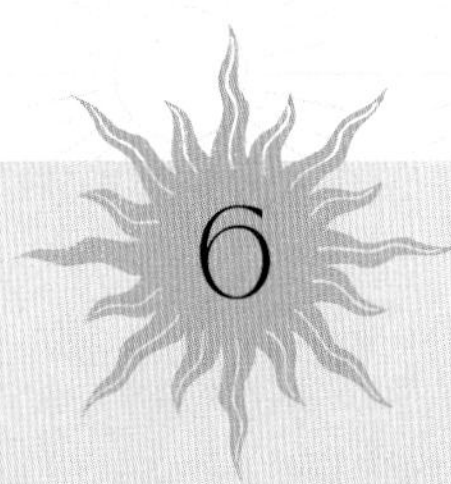


## HAVE A SOLSTICE MEAL

At this time of year, warming foods, hearty dishes, and spiced drinks are the order of the day. Winter vegetables, preserved fruits, and warming soups are traditional foods that will help to keep body and soul warm and happy at the darkest time of the year. Now is also the moment to open some of your preserved fruit from the Autumn Equinox if you have any, to bring a flavour of summer to this solstice celebration.

There is a lot of pressure around modern day winter festivities to create the perfect elaborate meal, but I think this time of year should be much gentler and more forgiving. If you want to host a Winter Solstice meal, I suggest asking family and friends to each bring a dish with them and put the focus instead on sharing food and spending time together, without the pressure of cooking a perfect meal. Light your table with gently flickering candles for Midwinter ambience, draw family and loved ones together, and raise a toast to the returning sun.

# GIVE A GIFT

Gifts have been exchanged around the Winter Solstice since the time of the Ancient Romans. In modern times, present giving has become the overwhelming focus of winter festivities, sometimes to the detriment of the real meaning of this time of the year, but it can still be nice to acknowledge the festival by sharing small gifts with loved ones.

If you'd like to give a solstice gift, below are a few ideas for seasonal nature-based gifts that can offer a reminder of the sun at this time of year.

These are all small, inexpensive ideas that you can probably find locally or even, in some cases, make yourself.

- Potted winter roses (hellebores) to bring light to winter gardens.
- Spiced shortbread to warm up with after a frosty winter walk (see Bake Warming Solstice Treats: Spiced Solstice Shortbread).
- Golden-coloured beeswax candles to light the dark (see Winter Solstice Crafts: Solstice Candles).
- Books about sun-drenched adventures for reading on long, dark nights – second-hand books make lovely gifts, in my opinion, and can be a more affordable option.
- Books about the solstice, or about the ancient civilizations that have celebrated and worshipped the sun throughout the centuries.
- A spiced and warming tea blend for staying cosy when the temperature drops outside.

# BAKE WARMING SOLSTICE TREATS

From spiced ginger cookies, to golden sun-breads, Winter Solstice baking is all about remembering the sun in the middle of winter, so recipes often include warming spices and sunshine citrus flavours. A clear and simple call for the sun in the depths of Midwinter. Here is a recipe for Spiced Solstice Shortbread, which is simple to make and delicious to eat at this time of year. It also makes an excellent solstice gift.

## SPICED SOLSTICE SHORTBREAD

This is baked in a circular tin in the shape of a sun, flavoured with orange zest and warming spices, and topped with a dusting of sparkling sugar.

### INGREDIENTS

- 115g (4oz) unsalted butter, softened
- 55g (2oz) caster (superfine) sugar
- Zest of 1 orange
- 180g (6oz) plain (all-purpose) flour
- ½ tsp ground mixed spice (apple pie spice)
- Granulated sugar, for decoration

**METHOD**

**1.** Preheat the oven to 160°C/140°C fan/Gas 3 (325°F). Line a 22cm (8½in) circular cake tin with baking (parchment) paper.

**2.** Cream the butter and sugar together in a bowl.

**3.** Add the orange zest, sift in the flour and ground mixed spice (apple pie spice), and mix together until smooth.

**4.** Gently turn out the dough and then press it into the cake tin, pushing the dough right to the edges and smoothing it out equally across the tin.

**5.** Use a knife to score the dough into triangle wedges, and then prick the surface with a fork. (As well as adding decoration, this allows the steam to escape and prevents the shortbread from bubbling up while cooking.)

**6.** Bake for 40–45 minutes or until a very light golden colour.

**7.** Remove from the oven, re-score the lines, then sprinkle with a little granulated sugar and leave to cool in the tin.

9

# TAKE A MIDWINTER WALK

There's something deeply peaceful about walking in woods or near trees at this time of the year. It can offer a moment of quiet and rest amid all the festive busyness, and there's a timelessness about being outside in nature. When daylight hours are so short it feels even more important to make the most of them and to get some sunlight on your skin for a few minutes each day. Taking a mindful walk at each of the solstices and equinoxes is a ritual that we will repeat throughout this book; you might want to take the same route as you did on your Autumn Equinox walk.

On your walk you might want to make a few notes of anything you spot, take some photos, or just simply absorb it all and enjoy it in peace.

## WHAT YOU MIGHT SPOT

Short days, long nights, and frost-covered landscapes; the time of the Winter Solstice is one of pared-back beauty, but there is still plenty to see and experience outdoors. There are inky skies studded with winter stars, woodlands cloaked with scarlet berries, and the spiced scent of winter evergreens to enjoy. Frosty days and bright winter sunlight are the best combination, so as soon as you get a day like that, get outside immediately!

On a frosty morning you should be able to clearly see the beautiful shapes and textures of the seedheads, grasses, and trees that remain in winter. Glossy evergreens shine out extra bright against a monochrome winter backdrop, as do bright red berries, making them easy to spot. If you're lucky, you might also spot some winter wildlife as overwintering species arrive to take the place of those that have migrated to warmer shores. Animal tracks can appear like magic in fresh snow, too, leaving a trail of clues and signs for those with sharp eyes.

Winter is also the absolute best time of year for stargazing, so if you're out walking at dusk, you might be in for a treat. This is due to several factors; the nights are obviously longer, so there is greater opportunity to stargaze than in the summer months, but the sky can also be clearer thanks to the crisp, cold air, which doesn't contain as much moisture as warm summer air, meaning that viewing conditions are much better. Winter also offers some of the clearest and brightest constellations of the year, as well as the most dramatic meteor showers, so there is plenty to see for those who make the effort to wrap up warm and step out into the winter night. The best times to see the stars are the days around each new moon when the sky is darkest.

And then, as you return home from your walk, you might catch a drift of woodsmoke in the air, with all its associated undertones of cosiness and fireside contentment, calling you back into the warm.

10

## UPDATE YOUR SEASONAL SHELF

It's time to update your seasonal collection, or nature altar, to reflect the new season. At this time of year you might like to bring in branches, evergreens, berries, or pinecones, and display them alongside a candle or two. You might also add a photo or illustration that sums up the spirit of this time of year, or display your favourite seasonal books. You could also include something that reminds you of the sun at this pivotal moment in the solar year: a decoration, ornament, or illustration.

As always, the beauty of a seasonal shelf or altar is that no two will be the same; yours will be completely bespoke and personal to you, so make sure to fill yours with things that bring you joy.

Children might like to bring in treasure from a winter walk to display on their own nature table. You might also want to help them add some toy winter animals, or some illustrated books that explain the festival of the solstice, as well as a representation or illustration of the sun. (See Winter Solstice Crafts for how to make a dried orange sun decoration.)

If you need some ideas to get started with your own seasonal shelf, or nature table, for the Winter Solstice you might like to bring in some of the following items:

- A small vase of winter berry-covered stems or evergreens.
- Photos, postcards, or pictures that represent the Winter Solstice for you. This could be a photo of a place that is special to you. Or it might be an illustration of a winter scene, or a line or two from a book or poem that brings up festive feelings for you.
- Seasonal books that tap into the cosiness and warmth of Midwinter.
- A decoration, drawing, or ornament that represents the sun.
- A candle in snowy white, forest green, or berry red.

# Winter Solstice Crafts

## DECORATE AN OUTDOOR TREE

While we're used to the idea of bringing a tree indoors, historically, in Germanic and Norse traditions, people would decorate evergreen trees outdoors as part of their Yule celebrations in a bid to encourage the spirit of the trees to return after the winter. Decorating a living tree outside, rather than bringing one indoors as we do today, is also a much more sustainable way to honour the season, and can be a really beautiful way to mark the holiday.

Choose a potted tree and place it outdoors, or use any other tree or bush already in the garden and decorate it with edible treats for the birds, such as popcorn strings, apple decorations, seedcakes, and pinecone feeders (see Autumn Equinox Crafts). You could also tie brightly coloured ribbons on to your tree as a temporary decoration. Worshipping and revering trees forms an important part of any pagan or nature-based festival, and taking the time to decorate a living tree with edible, natural decorations is a good way to gently connect to the outdoors at a time when we tend to be more inwardly focussed.

# SOLSTICE ICE SUNCATCHER

A beautiful way to decorate the outside of your home at this time of year is to make an ice decoration. This is a simple and natural festive decoration that can be made only on the coldest days and nights of the year. A glittering disc made entirely from ice that will catch the bright winter sunlight and reflect it, before melting away to nothing after use. These are great to make with children, or for a Midwinter party.

**YOU WILL NEED**

- Small circular dish or cupcake tray
- Berries and evergreen leaves
- Water
- Ribbon or string

**HERE'S HOW TO MAKE YOUR OWN SOLSTICE ICE SUNCATCHER**

**1.** Take a small circular dish (or to make several small decorations, you can use a cupcake tray).

**2.** Place a few red berries and evergreen leaves into the dish, or into each indentation in the cupcake tray.

**3.** Fill with water and place a loop of ribbon or string at the top of each one.

**4.** Place in a freezer, or leave outside overnight if you're expecting icy weather.

**5.** Once the water has frozen solid, remove your ice decoration from the tray.

**6.** Using the string or ribbon, hang it up outdoors somewhere it can catch the light to create a glowing disc of ice and berries.

**7.** After use, your decorations will melt away to nothing (leaving just the string or ribbon), making them the perfect sustainable solstice decoration.

# SOLSTICE CANDLES

Candles are an essential element of a solar solstice celebration, filling your home with Midwinter light. They also make excellent solstice gifts. Beeswax candles are my favourite type of candle; they're a beautiful golden colour and they produce a sweet, honey fragrance when lit. It's thought they also produce less toxins when they burn, and potentially even clean the air as they do so. For a solar festival, they're perfect.

Making your own solstice candles can be surprisingly straightforward, and if you follow the instructions here to make a rolled beeswax candle, there's no need to melt hot wax or use candle moulds. It's a quick and mess-free craft that is also safe for children to join in with.

**YOU WILL NEED**

- Pre-formed sheets of beeswax (you can buy these readily online)
- Scissors
- Ruler
- Candle wicks (again, look for pre-cut candle wicks online)

**HERE'S HOW TO MAKE YOUR OWN SOLSTICE CANDLES**

**1.** Ensure your beeswax is room temperature before use, as this will make it easier to roll. If it's too cold it may crack.

**2.** Lay out your beeswax sheet and cut it to size, if needed. The vertical edge will dictate the finished length of the candle and the width of the candle is determined by how many times you roll the beeswax sheet around the wick. As a guide, a 20 x 20cm (8 x 8in) square sheet will roll up to create one standard-sized dinner candle.

**3.** Place your candle wick along the vertical edge of the sheet, then cut it to leave 2cm (¾in) extra at the top.

**4.** Press the wick gently into the beeswax, then roll the edge of the sheet over so the wick is enclosed. Press firmly along the edge of the beeswax to seal in the wick.

**5.** Now gently roll the beeswax around the wick to form your candle shape.

**6.** When the candle is complete, press the edge of the sheet down firmly to seal it.

That's it. Your candle is now ready to light, or to give as a solstice gift.

You can experiment with different sizes, from dinner candles to small birthday-cake candles, by cutting the beeswax sheets to different sizes.

## DRIED ORANGE SUNCATCHER

Oranges are a traditional fruit to enjoy during Midwinter, they provide a reminder of warmer days to come, and their sweet, warm scent has become inextricably linked to Midwinter celebrations. Their round orange form is also a perfect visual representation of the sun, which makes them an excellent decoration for the Winter Solstice.

To make an orange suncatcher decoration you simply slice an orange into thin discs, dry them out to preserve them, then hang them up from a string or ribbon. When they're hung up at a window they allow the winter sun to shine through, catching and magnifying it, like natural stained glass, as well as filling your home with a spicy warm fragrance. Winter sun worship at its simplest and most pleasing.

**YOU WILL NEED**

- 1 orange
- Sharp knife
- Paper towels
- Baking tray
- Thin ribbon or string

### HERE'S HOW TO MAKE YOUR OWN ORANGE SUNCATCHER DECORATION

**1.** Preheat the oven to 140°C/120°C fan/ Gas 1 (275°F).

**2.** Take an orange and slice it into thin discs, around 6mm (¼in), with a sharp knife. Make sure to cut the orange through the middle (so the stem is in the centre) and not lengthways.

**3.** Pat each slice dry with a paper towel to remove as much of the juice as possible.

**4.** Spread the slices out on a baking tray and place them in the oven to dry out. Don't be tempted to turn the heat up to speed things up, as they will scorch and burn at a high temperature.

**5.** Check them every 20 minutes to see how they're drying, and turn them over to make sure they don't burn. Thinner slices will dry quicker than thicker ones, so if your slices are a little uneven, some might be ready before others.

**6.** Once the slices feel dry, take them out of the oven before they start to brown. This could take up to 2 hours in such a gentle heat. Your kitchen will smell beautifully festive the entire time, though!

**7.** Leave them to cool on a wire rack.

**8.** Once they're cool and dry, make a hole in the top of each one and hang them from the thin ribbon or string.

**9.** Place them near a window to allow them to catch and reflect the winter sunlight. You could also hang them on your solstice tree.

# Spring Equinox

# What is the Spring Equinox?

The Spring Equinox occurs when, for a brief moment, the Sun is directly above the Earth's Equator. At this moment the Earth is tilted neither away from nor towards the Sun. This means that during the equinox there will be approximately 12 hours of day and 12 hours of night.

The Spring Equinox falls between 19 and 21 March, exactly halfway between the Winter Solstice and Summer Solstice. In the Northern Hemisphere, the March equinox marks the astronomical start of spring.

The Spring Equinox marks the start of moving towards the light and is a time to celebrate the sun's returning strength. From this point on, each day will become longer as the light returns and we head towards the longest day of the year at the Summer Solstice.

# How Does it Affect Us?

For many people the return of the light at the Spring Equinox after the long winter months is joyful and deeply energizing. Those of us who desperately missed the sun over the past few months will breathe a big sigh of relief as we feel fresh energy and life flowing back into us. Even those of us who actually quite enjoyed the rest and peace of the winter may be about ready to step out of hibernation and emerge into the light when the equinox arrives.

Ever since the shortest day on the Winter Solstice, the number of hours of sunlight per day have been slowly but steadily increasing, and in the cycle of the year, the equinox is a time of growth and rebirth. The natural world reacts in a clear and definite way to these extra hours of sunlight: birds start building nests and laying eggs; the first lambs are being born; fresh green shoots are pushing up from the ground; and March hares start racing around in the fields.

Many of us will also respond in a significant way to the returning light. The increasing hours of daylight around the time of the equinox give us a steadily growing window each day in which to absorb sunlight, which may result in increased energy levels and optimism. With the gradual return of fertility to the land outside, we might also feel a flow of new creative energy within ourselves too, with fresh ideas and inspiration bubbling up at this time of year. Everything suddenly feels hopeful, fresh, and alive, and if spring is particularly your favourite season, you will probably be feeling as light and happy as the newborn lambs in the fields.

There is also a clarity and a freshness to the light in spring that is completely unique to this time of year, and after several months of winter, we feel the return of this light most keenly. The weather in March can still be chilly, but those little moments when the wind suddenly drops and the sun feels warm on our face for the first time in months are an absolute tonic. As the first shoots and flowers push their way up through the soil to greet the spring sunshine, we might react in much the same way, turning our faces up to the warm spring sun to soak up every last drop. Sun worship at its most simple and instinctive!

The colours of the landscape around us are predominantly yellow and white at the Spring Equinox, too. Plump golden dandelions, buttery-coloured daffodils, and pure white tree blossom can all be found in the landscape this month, providing bright points of light that feel like bottled sunshine.

The rituals and celebrations that we have woven around the equinox reflect this growing optimism and desire for a fresh start. As a festival day, the equinox is an opportunity to welcome and encourage the return of the light, to cleanse away any sleepy winter energy and make way for new spring growth. The Spring Equinox is also an excellent time to set goals and make resolutions. If, like me, you refuse to make New Year resolutions in January when we are, after all, still in the depths of Midwinter, you might find that the equinox feels like a *much* more appropriate time for these. There's a purposeful energy around the equinox that feels like a proper "New Year" start.

There is no rush though; despite this growing sense of energy, this is still a gentle shift and a slow awakening. Some of us might need a little longer to be coaxed back out into the light after a cosy winter of hibernation, and that's okay. I am always a little reluctant to leave my den when spring rolls around; I've become very good at embracing the dark months of the year. So I think it's wise to approach the Spring Equinox at your own pace. For some of us this will be a gentle shift, and we might need to treat ourselves kindly as we adjust.

Right now we are poised exactly between the sleepy peace of Midwinter and the solar-powered energy of Midsummer. With light and darkness levels perfectly balanced on this day, we can hopefully feel a mirrored sense of balance and energy within ourselves. The equinox is a time for taking a breath and gathering ourselves before we step forward into the light half of the year.

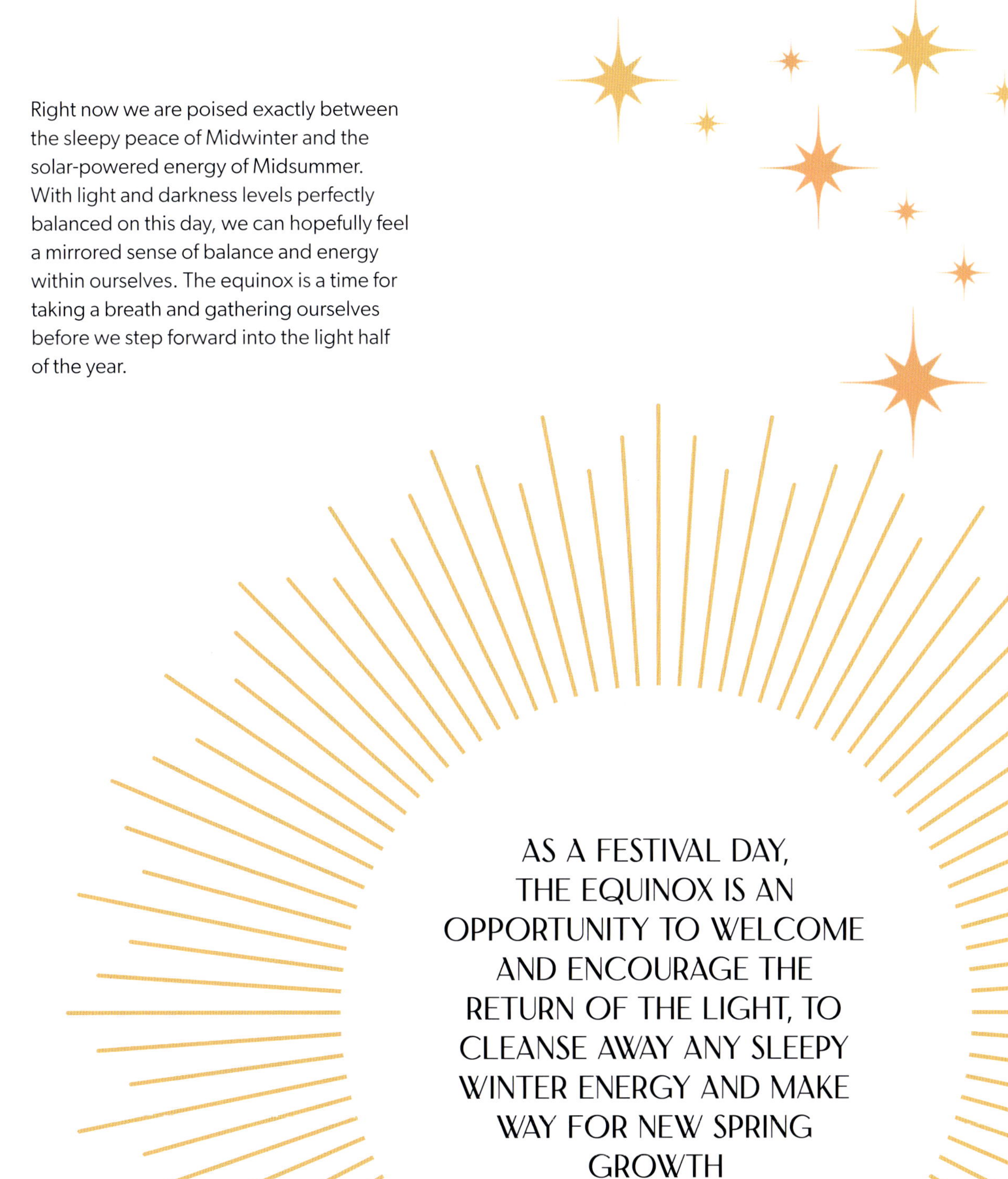

AS A FESTIVAL DAY, THE EQUINOX IS AN OPPORTUNITY TO WELCOME AND ENCOURAGE THE RETURN OF THE LIGHT, TO CLEANSE AWAY ANY SLEEPY WINTER ENERGY AND MAKE WAY FOR NEW SPRING GROWTH

# Ancient Magic and Folklore of the Spring Equinox

There is a still and deep magic to the equinoxes that provides a quiet counterbalance to the showier drama of the solstices. While the solstices leave a clear trail of clues back to ancient times, providing set rituals and traditions to follow, there are fewer records of how the equinoxes were celebrated in pre-Christian times. Instead we have to piece together clues and fragments to find a thread to follow back to our ancestors. But you can still find traces of magic hovering around these days when you start to look for them.

Ancient monuments to equinox sun worship can be found scattered all over the world, from Mexico to Cambodia to Ireland, indicating these were dates of considerable significance to many cultures.

While there was likely to have been a practical element to these early sundials, the beautiful temple-like construction of these monuments marks them out as a place of spiritual worship, too.

The ancient Maya city of Chichén Itzá in Mexico, for example, draws visitors each year on the equinox to watch as the sun sets over the largest pyramid in the city, El Castillo, or The Temple of Kukulkán. As the sun sets, it casts a shadow along a stone staircase, creating the optical illusion of a snake slithering down the steps. This beautiful shadow is believed to be a representation of the feathered serpent god Kukulkán as he descends the steps to visit the temple at this precise moment each year.

Another example of ancient solar architecture is the Angkor Wat temple in Cambodia. The pinnacle of the temple's central tower has been designed to perfectly align with the rising sun at the Spring Equinox. This means that when dawn breaks at the equinox it provides the illusion of the sun resting for a moment directly on top of the tower.

In more recent history, the Spring Equinox has been used to mark the start of the farming season; a time of huge importance for agricultural communities. After the dark winter months the returning sun at the Spring Equinox would have given a clear and practical signal that the time was coming to plant crops, prepare the land and mark the return of the farming season. For cultures that relied heavily on agriculture for their survival, every little marker of spring would have been an occasion to celebrate the return of the sun.

# Sun God of the Season

## INTI

Inti the Inca Sun God was thought to have been a prominent figure in ancient Inca civilization. As a solar god he would have the power to bring light and warmth to the earth and to make crops grow, so he was closely linked to agriculture and prosperity.

Gold appears to have been associated with the mythology and worship of Inti, with the rays of the sun seen as pouring gold over the earth. Like many sun gods, Inti was also closely linked to the moon goddess, his sister Mama-Quilla, and according to the mythology she mirrors his rays of gold with her own tears of pure silver.

Much Inca architecture was designed with the solar and lunar cycles in mind, and temples and shrines were dedicated to Inti in order to appease and celebrate him. If he was happy, it was thought the sun would shine and crops would grow. If he was unhappy, it was thought there would be a bad harvest, and sacrifices must be made to appease him. Solar eclipses could also be considered a sign of his anger.

# 10 Modern Rituals to Welcome the Spring

Ready to celebrate? Today the Spring Equinox is regarded as the astronomical start of spring, and celebrations associated with it have a focus on fertility, growth, and rebirth. Here are a few ideas of how to mark the day and fill it with a little equinox magic, from refreshing dips to cheerful decorations and a beautiful equinox sunrise. As a festival day, this is an opportunity to welcome and encourage the return of the light, to sweep away any sleepy winter energy and set gentle intentions for the year ahead.

Whether you just want to light a candle and gently welcome the dawn, or whether you feel inspired to declutter your home from top to bottom, how you spend the day is up to you. Sometimes just carrying around the knowledge that it is the Spring Equinox can make the day feel special. Whatever you decide to do, I hope you have a wonderful day, full of bright, fresh, solar energy.

THIS IS AN OPPORTUNITY TO WELCOME AND ENCOURAGE THE RETURN OF THE LIGHT, TO SHRUG OFF THE HIBERNATION OF WINTER AND SET GENTLE INTENTIONS FOR THE YEAR AHEAD

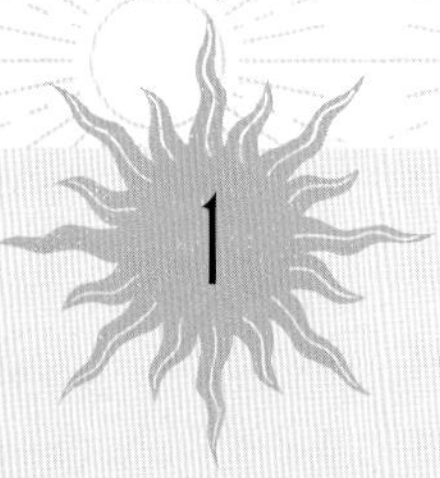

# GREET THE DAWN

Once again, we will start the new solar season by greeting the sunrise on the morning of the Spring Equinox, just as our ancestors have been doing for centuries.

The Spring Equinox marks the start of returning light, so now is a time to give thanks for the winter season and to acknowledge the sun's growing strength. From this point on, each day will become longer as we head towards the longest day of the year at the Summer Solstice. But now is the moment to offer gratitude for the past few months, as well as offering up your hopes and wishes for the coming season.

To make this into a ritual, as the sun rises above the horizon, take a moment to give thanks for the rest and peace of the winter months, acknowledge the start of a new phase of energy, and set your intentions for the new season ahead.

These intentions might be goal driven, such as completing a creative project, or they might be broader in scope, such as looking after your health or spending more time outside in nature. Make sure whatever you choose feels positive and joyful to you and not restrictive or negative. To focus on exactly what is important to you, close your eyes, take a deep breath, and try to visualize the year ahead. What would bring you joy and what would you like to turn your energy towards? Pick one or two clear goals and set them as your intention. Then breathe out slowly and release the intention out into the world.

# PLANT SEEDS

Many believe the Spring Equinox is a powerful time to plant seeds, so you could take this opportunity to get some seeds into the ground if conditions are suitable. The rapidly returning light levels will make quick work of any seedlings you place on a warm windowsill, giving them a powerful kickstart. Any planting plans you made over the winter will come into practice now, as we move from the gentle planning phase of the Winter Solstice to the action-focused energy of the Spring Equinox. Many indoor vegetable and flower seeds can be sown on a warm windowsill now and if the ground is warm enough, some might be able to be planted outdoors, but this will depend on the soil type and weather conditions where you live. Even if you have to wait a few more weeks for the ground to warm up, you can still get outside during the equinox to get your hands into the earth and feel some spring sun on your face as you get your seed beds and outdoor space ready.

To choose which seeds to plant, think about the kind of garden you'd like to cultivate in the year ahead and plant intentionally for this. Do you want to grow a vegetable garden to sustain you through the summer and autumn, or would a flower garden bring you more joy? Are you drawn to herbs, or do you want to try some quick-growing seeds to get children involved and engaged? Choose your seeds carefully and align them with your intentions and goals for the year ahead.

## SET NEW YEAR INTENTIONS

Some people consider the Spring Equinox to be the start of their New Year, and there is definitely a New Year energy in the air at this time of year. So if any creative plans have been ticking over in the back of your mind, now is the time to set intentions and put them into practice. If you're not sure exactly where to start, small steps are perfectly acceptable at this time of year; you don't have to throw yourself straight into it. You could clear some desk space, dust off some art materials, or research some classes.

The returning light at the equinox can also help to shine a light on the path ahead, so if you're looking for a little guidance, use this opportunity to get everything in place, then relax and wait for creative inspiration to strike! This might also feel like the right time to do something physical to awaken all the senses after the sleepiness of the winter. Taking a walk or doing some gardening can often help to shake ideas and thoughts free, or help you to see things from a different perspective, if needed.

# SPRING CLEAN

There's a purposeful energy to spring, and an irresistible urge to clean and declutter often creeps up on us around this time. If you want to let go of some of the restful energy of winter and welcome a fresh new year, pick just one or two of these jobs to bring your home and your mind into the new season, so you can move forward into spring with a lighter step.

- Clean your windows to symbolically and literally let in the increasing daylight.
- Briefly open all the windows to let some fresh spring air into your home.
- Dust window blinds and give curtains a good shake or vacuum to allow a clean flow of energy to come through the windows.
- Tidy up home office spaces, tackle paperwork, and clear your desk.
- Clear any clutter from the main walkways in your home.
- Bring more lightweight spring clothes to the front of the wardrobe.
- Dust any light fittings and shades to maximize light inside the home.
- Get any outdoor furniture ready for warmer days on the horizon.
- Clean your doormats to literally and symbolically sweep away any dirt and mud that collected over winter.
- Refresh, clean, and store bulky winter bedding, shake out blankets and quilts, and air them on the line if you get a sunny day.
- And finally... **DECLUTTER**
  If the thought of decluttering is a bit overwhelming, or you just don't have time to do a big clear out, try doing one piece at a time. Leave a box by the front door and every day take a minute to place one item in the box to donate or give away.

# BRING SPRING FLOWERS INTO YOUR HOME

After all that spring cleaning, now is the time to bring in some spring flowers to celebrate the new season and weave in some of that lovely optimistic colour and life. Bunches of daffodils are the surest sign of spring, and their bright saturated colour can feel like a tonic after the long months of darkness. Fill vases with them and place them all around your home to enjoy their colour and scent. Some early tulips will be starting to flower at the end of March too, and these make for lovely equinox flower displays, if you can find them.

Flowers have long been imbued with symbolism and meaning, from ancient myths to the Victorian practice of 'floriography' (also known as the 'language of flowers'). In *floriography* the spring daffodil was thought to represent chivalry or respect when given as a gift (a more cheerful interpretation than the ancient Greek myth of Narcissus, which warns of excess vanity), while red tulips are thought to have symbolized true love. Daisies are almost universally linked to rebirth and new beginnings; they can also be woven into chains for protection, or even used in love divination ('he loves me, he loves me not').

If you want to grow your own cut flowers next spring, make a note now of the bulbs you will need to plant in autumn to make this happen, and write yourself a reminder to plant them at the Autumn Equinox. I think of the two equinoxes as intrinsically linked, and I like the idea of taking actions now that will come to fruition at the Autumn Equinox and vice versa.

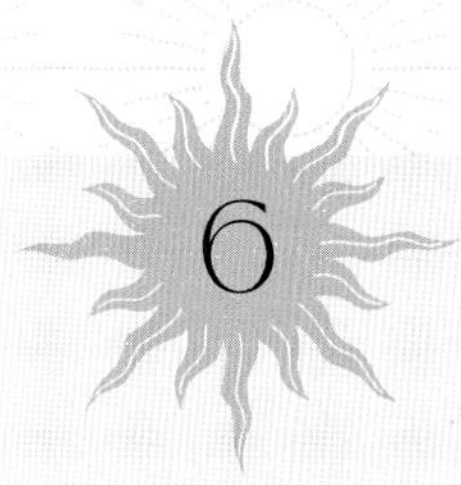


## TAKE A CLEANSING DIP

The equinox is a time for cleansing, refreshing, and washing away any of the dustiness of winter. This can relate to your home, your mind, or more literally, your body, with a ritual bath or refreshing swim. There's something about the increasing hours of daylight at this time of year that make me feel drawn to the water. I see the first rays of warm spring sunshine beckoning through the window and immediately start thinking about taking a dip somewhere outdoors. It's usually far too cold to do that of course, but walking near water at the equinox and perhaps dipping your hands in some water, if it's safe to do so, feels very invigorating at this time of year.

You can also bring your cleansing ritual closer to home and immerse yourself in a warm indoor bath to mark the equinox. Add refreshing bath oils or a herb sachet to the water, and as you bathe, imagine all the dustiness and sleepiness of winter being washed away. Then as you step out of the bath, imagine leaving the winter behind and stepping into the new season.

# CELEBRATE FRESH AND HERBY FLAVOURS

After several delicious months of warming wintry foods and festive flavours, the equinox feels like the right time to introduce some fresher foods to match the bright energy of spring. Rosemary bread and lemon and orange cakes all start to call my name at this time of year; anything with a citrusy, zesty flavour feels appropriate. Now is also a great time to make some fresh herbal teas. Nettle, for example, can be a natural energy booster and is abundant in gardens and hedgerows right now. The dried or fresh leaves of nettle make a pleasingly green cup of tea that tastes exactly like fresh, clean hedgerows.

Below is a recipe for refreshing lemon cakes that particularly reflects this energizing time of year. These would go perfectly with a cup of herbal tea.

## LEMON SUN CAKES

Mark the returning light with the bright, sunshine flavour of these fresh lemon equinox cakes. This recipe makes a tray of around 12 small sun cakes, each topped with a fresh and tangy lemon glaze. As you stir your cake mixture you could also visualize your goals and intentions for the year and stir in a wish for the year ahead.

### INGREDIENTS

- 110g (4oz) caster (superfine) sugar
- 110g (4oz) butter
- 2 eggs
- 1 tsp baking powder
- Grated zest of 1 large unwaxed lemon
- 110g (4oz) self-raising flour

#### FOR THE LEMON GLAZE

- Juice of 1 large lemon
- 40g (1½oz) granulated sugar
- Candied lemon peel (optional)

**METHOD**

**1.** Preheat the oven to 180°C/160°C fan/Gas 4 (350°F).

**2.** Combine the sugar, butter, eggs, and baking powder in a bowl. Add the grated lemon zest, sift in the flour, and mix well using a hand mixer or in a stand mixer until you get a smooth-textured batter.

**3.** Pour the batter into 12 individual paper muffin or cake cases.

**4.** Place in the centre of the oven and bake for 10–15 minutes or until they just start to turn a golden colour on top.

**5.** To test if your cakes are done, gently press the top of a cake – if it springs back up, it's done. If an indent remains, then cook it for a few more minutes and test again.

**6.** Turn the cakes out onto a wire rack and allow to cool in their cases.

**7.** While the cakes are still warm, make the lemon glaze by mixing the lemon juice with the granulated sugar in a bowl and stirring until dissolved.

**8.** Poke a few small holes in the top of each cake and pour the lemon glaze over each cake while still warm, allowing it to soak in.

**9.** Once cool, top with candied lemon peel, if using.

# LOOK FOR BALANCE

Just as in autumn, the solar balance offers an opportunity to consider what is in balance in your life and reflect on what might need adjusting. We're going to mark this moment of equilibrium by repeating the rebalancing ritual we completed at the Autumn Equinox.

Repeating this ritual at each of the equinoxes can offer you the chance to refocus on what is important to you, what you want to invite more of into your life, and what you would like to let go of.

So now is the time to look back at your lists from the autumn and see if they've pulled a little more into balance. Celebrate any achievements, and refocus on anything you want to work on as we head into spring.

This ritual is just for you, so relax, write intuitively, and enjoy the process. There's no right or wrong way to do it and no one will be marking your work at the end! It is a ritual just for you, so just relax, write intuitively, and enjoy the process.

## SPRING EQUINOX "REBALANCING" RITUAL

### YOU WILL NEED

- Autumn Equinox rebalancing ritual lists (see Autumn Equinox: Look for Balance)
- 2 pieces of A4 (letter) paper
- Pen
- Scissors
- Magazines, catalogues, or other visual materials for mood boarding
- Glue stick

**METHOD**

**1.** Start by taking your two lists from the Autumn Equinox. You should have a list of things you want more of in your life and a list of things you'd like to let go of or reduce. Take a moment to read through them and see how you feel. Have they started to balance out a little? Have you managed to let go of things that no longer feel good to you and invite more positive things into your life? Are they in need of a refresh?

**2.** On a fresh piece of paper write a new list of all the things you'd like to invite more of into your life. You can carry over ideas and images from your previous mood board if they still apply, or you can start a completely fresh one, whatever feels right for you. As before, we're going to illustrate this list with visuals, so cut out and add images to create a mood board of lovely things that you'd like to invite into your life.

**3.** When you've finished this, replace the one you made at the Autumn Equinox, putting your spring mood board somewhere you can see it easily every day. You want to focus your attention on this list of things that feel important and deeply personal to you.

**4.** Now, on a second piece of paper, write down anything that you feel takes up too much time in your life or that you would like to let go of. Again, you can look at your Autumn Equinox list and carry over some of the same themes from that one, but hopefully some of them can be removed. As before though, this list doesn't get the mood board treatment. You don't want to focus any creative energy on things you want to reduce or get rid of. So just write a simple list.

**5.** Tuck this second list away somewhere out of sight, but keep it safe and we'll check in again with it at the Autumn Equinox.

That's it. Now there's nothing more to do, or worry about. You are continuing on your journey towards letting go of the things that don't serve you in your life; and with more practise you will find it easier to identify the things that are truly important to you and to release the burden of those things you no longer need.

# TAKE A SPRING EQUINOX WALK

After the dark, restful months of winter we probably all feel the need to shake off some of the inertia and get back outdoors again. This moment of perfect balance is a great time to get outside and celebrate the sun's returning strength as the land around us moves into spring.

Taking a mindful walk at each of the solstices and equinoxes is a ritual we are repeating throughout the year to help join up the seasons and notice how much the landscape around us is changing with each new solar festival. On your Spring Equinox walk you might want to make a few notes of anything you notice or take some photos; if you'd rather, you can, of course, just simply absorb it all and enjoy it in peace.

## WHAT YOU MIGHT SPOT

March is a month of dramatic change, sweeping in with an icy breeze but ending with all the colour and optimism of early spring. Light levels increase at a pace, and everything brims with promise. It's a season of glittering spring flowers, bright, cold rivers, and cool, clean air.

Trees should be starting to bud or leaf up now, and native woodland flowers will start to emerge underneath them. The first blossoms will soon start to cover trees and hedgerows. You're also likely to spot plenty of sunshine-bright daffodils, daisies, and dandelions dotted amongst the grass. From now on the landscape around you will rapidly fill with flowers, colour, and scent.

Early risers will also notice the increasing volume and intensity of birdsong, which peaks shortly after the equinox; if you're up early you should be able to hear native songbirds making the most of the quiet still mornings to sing at the top of their voices. It's also nest-building time for many birds, so if you're very quiet and very lucky, you might spot some nesting activity.

Migratory birds that overwintered in warmer countries should be returning to your shores any day now as the breeding season gets underway. Woodland animals such as foxes, badgers, and squirrels will all start raising their young around now, too, so keep an eye out when walking near wild animal habitats. The first of this year's lambs will be appearing out in the fields as well. All in all, it's an exciting time to be outdoors, full of unfurling energy and life.

# UPDATE YOUR SEASONAL SHELF

It's time to update your seasonal collection, or nature altar, to reflect the new season. At this time of year it's all about early spring treasures. You might like to bring in blossom, leaves, or a small vase of spring flowers to display this month. You could also add a photo or illustration that sums up the spirit of this time of year, or display your favourite spring books. You might also include something that reminds you of the sun: a decoration, ornament, or illustration.

If you're helping children to make their own nature table, you might want to help them to make a display with some flowers, leaves, or blossom, alongside some illustrated books that explain the Spring Equinox.

If you need some ideas to get started with your own seasonal shelf, or nature table, for the Spring Equinox you might like to bring in some of the following items:

- A small vase of spring flowers; dandelions, daffodils, daisies.
- Spring treasures that you've picked up on a nature walk; shells, stones, a beautiful piece of bark, a fallen piece of blossom...

- Photos, postcards, or pictures that sum up the Spring Equinox for you. This could be a photo of a place that is special to you, such as a favourite walk or beach. Or it might be an illustration of a spring flower, or a line or two from a book or poem that brings up happy feelings for you.
- Seasonal books that tap into spring energy.
- A representation of the sun. This might be a yellow crystal, a small image, or perhaps a charm, just something to remind you of the growing strength of the sun at this time of year.
- A candle in white, yellow, or green.
- Seedlings. If you planted seeds for the Equinox, place a pot or tray of these on your nature shelf to bring some of that emerging spring energy with them. If you're planning to plant seeds a little later in the season, place the packet of seeds on your shelf as a reminder of your intentions.
- A pot of fresh herbs. At this time of new growth, placing a pot of zingy-scented herbs on your nature shelf will really bring it to life. Try something with a strong, fresh scent such as mint so, when you brush the leaves, it will release a burst of bright scent.

# Spring Equinox Crafts

## SPRING EQUINOX WREATH

Hanging a wreath in spring colours on your front door is the perfect way to signal a new season has begun. The circular shape is an ancient symbol of balance and represents the steady and reliable turning of the year. The shape is also, obviously, a visual nod to the sun, so making seasonal wreaths is a nice way of repeating this solar motif throughout the year.

A Spring Equinox wreath helps to signify the start of the growing and flowering season. You can buy a pre-made wreath if you are short on time, but they are quite simple and enjoyable to make yourself if you have the inclination. Start with a pre-bought rattan wreath base. My advice is to go larger than you think with this. A large wreath will make more of a generous impact on a front door than a tiny little one, and you can reuse it all year round. If you buy a plain wreath base you can then update it for each of the solar festivals in this book.

**YOU WILL NEED**

- Spring foliage
- Florist wire and/or twine
- Wreath base – this can be rattan, wire, or willow
- Flowers – fresh, dried, or felt
- Ribbon
- Small spring decorations, such as decorative eggs, or wooden or metal ornaments of suns, hares, flowers, eggs, or other equinox motifs

**HERE'S HOW TO MAKE YOUR OWN SPRING EQUINOX WREATH**

**1.** Tie small handfuls of your spring foliage into bunches with the florist wire.

**2.** Attach these to your wreath base one by one with more of the florist wire or twine to build up a green base. Leave the tops untied so they can spring away from the circle to add some movement. You can completely cover the wreath with these foliage bunches, or you can cover just the lower third or half of the wreath, depending on your time and inclination.

**3.** Once you have the base of greenery, add in small flowers for colour. Fresh flowers will obviously have a very short shelf life once they have been cut, so you might want to use dried flowers for this, or felt flowers if you want your wreath to last longer than a day or two.

**4.** Tie short lengths of colourful ribbon to your wreath for an extra burst of vibrant spring colour.

**5.** Add in your small spring decorations: anything that signals spring and new life to you; you could try wooden or metal ornaments of spring motifs such as suns, hares, flowers, and eggs, for example.

**6.** Add a length of brightly coloured ribbon to the top to create a hanging loop.

**7.** Display your wreath on your front door for all to see and enjoy.

## COLOURFUL INDOOR "TREE"

One of my favourite spring traditions is to make a colourful indoor "tree" in a vase, using branches decorated with colourful ribbons and small spring decorations. It's a lovely nod to the decorated trees of the Winter Solstice and it's very simple to make. You can turn your act of decorating into a mini spring ritual, too, by using the opportunity to think about your wishes for the upcoming season. At this optimistic time of year it's a creative way to help focus on any plans and hopes for the year ahead. It's also a great way to share the season with others, as you can offer family and friends the chance to tie on their own ribbon or decoration and make a wish too. Children always love getting involved with this activity.

**YOU WILL NEED**

- 3–5 large branches (buy seasonal branches of foliage locally or cut some branches from your garden, if you are able)
- Large sturdy jug or vase with a heavy base (add stones to weigh it down, if needed)
- Colourful ribbons
- Spring motif decorations, such as hollow wooden eggs, hares, flowers, sun motifs
- Fabric, felt flowers, colourful material scraps, or feathers

**HERE'S HOW TO MAKE YOUR OWN INDOOR TREE**

**1.** Arrange your branches in your jug or vase. You need only a few branches, but they do need to be quite sturdy. Bare branches work just as well as branches with leaves.

**2.** Tie on colourful ribbons and small, lightweight decorations such as hollow wooden eggs, hares, flowers, or sun motifs.

**3.** You could also tie on scraps of brightly patterned fabric, felt flowers, or feathers; anything that says "spring" to you.

**4.** As you tie each decoration to a branch, make a wish for the new season and think about what you would like to invite into your life in the coming months.

**5.** Place the tree somewhere central in your home where everyone can see it and enjoy it.

**6.** Leave a few ribbons or decorations in a bowl near the tree and invite any visitors to add one and make an equinox wish.

# PLANT SUNFLOWER SEEDS

If you have time to plant only one type of seed this spring, make it a sunflower seed. They are the most joyful, beautiful tribute to the sun and they grow astonishingly fast. Young sunflower buds are also heliotropic (from the Greek *helios*, meaning "sun"), which means they move their heads to follow the course of the sun across the sky each day. Every night they return to face east to greet the rising sun the next morning and once the sunflowers mature, they remain fixed facing east to greet the rising sun.

If you plant your seeds now you should have a garden full of bright yellow suns by late summer. Then at the Autumn Equinox you can gather their seeds (you will have hundreds from each sunflower) and save them to plant again next spring.

**YOU WILL NEED**

- Pots (approx. 7.5cm/3in)
- Peat-free compost
- Sunflower seeds
- Propagator lid or plastic bag

**HERE'S HOW TO PLANT YOUR SUNFLOWER SEEDS**

**1.** Fill a few small pots with compost.

**2.** Push one seed into each pot and press it about 1cm (¾in) below the surface.

**3.** Cover with a propagator lid or a clear plastic bag with a few ventilation holes and place them on a warm windowsill.

**4.** Water well, then keep well watered.

**5.** Remove the plastic cover once the seedlings emerge.

**Note:** When the seedlings are around 30cm (12in) tall, you can plant them outside: place them somewhere sunny and protected from slugs and snails and stake them as they grow to help support the heavy flower heads.

# PAINT EQUINOX EGGS

Eggs have been celebrated as a symbol of spring for centuries, as they represent fertility, creation, and new life at this time of the returning sun. Wooden or paper mache eggs make lovely decorations that can be reused each year, and they are a nice way to bring this spring symbol into your home. You can buy these pre-painted, or you can buy them unpainted and decorate them yourself.

If you fancy painting some yourself as an equinox activity, here are a few ideas to try:

- Use natural dyes such as turmeric or beetroot to colour your eggs.
- Decorate them with treasures from the garden such as pressed flowers and dried leaves.
- Draw or paint natural symbols such as birds and bees to symbolize new life.
- Decoupage the eggs with thin layers of brightly patterned tissue paper or wrapping paper.
- Wrap the eggs in a square of cheerful patterned fabric, tying it at the top.
- Use nature motif stencils or stickers to delicately cover the surface with patterns.

Once you've finished you can hang the decorated eggs in a window, or from a vase of branches for a cheerful table display. You could also give them as equinox gifts. And finally, if you fancy giving egg balancing a go, this is the day to do it, as legend says that on the equinox an egg can be balanced on one end!

Summer
Solstice

# What is the Summer Solstice?

The Summer Solstice occurs when the Earth is at its maximum tilt towards the Sun, creating the longest day and the shortest night of the year.

In the Northern Hemisphere this falls between 20 and 22 June and it marks the official start of astronomical summer. However some believe the solstice actually marks the midpoint of the season, hence the name "Midsummer", which is also used to describe this time of year.

After this point the balance will start to shift towards the dark again, and the amount of sunlight each day will decrease slowly as the wheel turns towards the Autumn Equinox.

**A note on Midsummer:** The time around the solstice is more commonly known as Midsummer in some cultures – particularly Scandinavian countries. Across Europe, "Midsummer" or "solstice" celebrations generally take place somewhere between 19 and 24 June depending on local customs. As such, throughout this chapter the terms *Summer Solstice* and *Midsummer* can be considered interchangeable.

# How Does it Affect Us?

In the solar year, the Summer Solstice is undeniably *the big event*. At the time of the solstice, the days are bright and long, the natural world is lush with greenery and flowers, and as we reach the longest day the extra hours of sunlight can have a dramatic effect on us.

We are more likely to get out of bed earlier, with sunlight pushing in through the curtains early, and more likely to stay up later too, as the long, warm evenings invite us to linger outside past our bedtime. The long hot days around the solstice give us a bigger window each day in which to absorb sunlight, allowing us a greater opportunity to produce vitamin D and potentially boosting our energy levels. We might not feel the need to sleep as much at this time of year either, thanks to the short, light nights. This change can be felt most keenly in the most northerly countries where the sun barely sets at this time of year and the solstice is known as the night of the midnight sun.

Sunlight has a particular intensity to it at the solstice too; in contrast to the pale light of spring or the rich warmth of autumn, light at the solstice is sharp and clear, throwing its searching gaze across everything. Colours are saturated, contrasts are bright, and everything is turned up to full power. There's also something new to see wherever you look this month: gardens are busy, hedgerows are teeming with life and it feels as if there's a constant hum of energy in the air. The pull to be outside is strong and when doors and windows are left open, the boundaries between inside and out start to blur. At this time of year, a connection to the natural world is easy and simple. Meals can be eaten outside, parks and playgrounds are full, woods are cool and inviting, and the invitation to play is everywhere.

In the cycle of the year, this is a time of activity and optimism. Topped up by solar power as we reach the brightest point of the year, we may find we have much more energy and enthusiasm for socializing, playing, and travelling than at other times in the year. In direct contrast to the introspection of the dark half of the year, the Summer Solstice is a time to indulge the extrovert side of ourselves. We are more likely to live in the moment, say yes to new opportunities and experiences, and make memories to take with us into the winter months. Even when the sun does eventually set, the nights are still warm at this time of the year, so there is a temptation to stay outside long into the summer night, listening to the crickets chirping and feeling the warm evening settle around us.

For our ancestors, the long sunny days of summer were traditionally a time to get things done. After long winter months of rest, the summer was an opportunity to make deals, negotiate, barter, and socialize, and we may find ourselves following the same patterns of behaviour during the summer months, too. There is also, running underneath all of this, an awareness that after this moment, the balance will start to slowly but surely shift again towards the dark. As impossible as it seems at the height of summer, each day following the solstice will be shorter than the last. So there is an urgency to the celebrations and a need to enjoy the outdoors while we can. That said, this time of year can also be very intense and overwhelming and some of us might find it easier to manage than others. It's important to find time to cool down, pace ourselves, and find ways to navigate this time of intense heat and activity. If this time of year is exhausting for you, then it's important to give yourself pockets of time to step away and take some time out.

This time of strong solar energy has also historically been a time of deep magic. Ancient monuments to sun worship called our ancestors to celebrate and observe this day and it is considered to be a potent time to harvest and store herbs, perform solar rituals and tap into the magical or spiritual realm.

Many stories and myths around the Summer Solstice tell of otherworldly happenings unfolding on this night; of fairies and spirits roaming free and of the ensuing mayhem. *A Midsummer Night's Dream* by Shakespeare is a classic example of this strange, heightened state of being that swirls around the solstice. Knowing what we do now about the impact that light can have on our internal body clocks and mood, it's quite possible that the feverish rush of energy described in books and plays can be linked to this huge dose of sunlight that our bodies experience. The strong solar energy makes us act in impulsive and extroverted ways, and perhaps makes us more open to magical and mystical possibilities.

TOPPED UP BY SOLAR POWER AS WE REACH THE BRIGHTEST POINT OF THE YEAR, WE MAY FIND WE HAVE MUCH MORE ENERGY AND ENTHUSIASM FOR SOCIALIZING, PLAYING, AND TRAVELLING THAN AT OTHER TIMES IN THE YEAR

# Ancient Magic and Folklore of the Summer Solstice

The Summer Solstice is completely woven through with magic and mystery. Because the sun appears to "stand still" in the sky for a few days around the solstice, it has long been seen as a strange and otherworldly time, where normal laws of nature were suspended and magical things could happen. Many civilizations and cultures have created rituals and festivals to mark this day, and it has long been considered a time when the veil between the spirit world and the real world becomes thin, allowing mischief and magic to slip through.

Ancient monuments to sun worship at the solstice can be found across the world, with one of the most well-known being Stonehenge in the UK. This is still a gathering place for people to celebrate today, with many staying up all night to greet the dawn on the longest day of the year. Standing in the centre of the stones at the solstice you can see the sun rise above the stones exactly as it has done for thousands of years.

This time of year has historically been particularly celebrated in Scandinavian countries, where the difference in light levels is most marked and the sun barely sets. From long Midsummer feasts under

the midnight sun to maypole dancing, flower crown wearing, and lighting bonfires, many of these Scandinavian traditions have been adapted and borrowed by other countries over time, forming the basis of our Summer Solstice traditions in the Northern Hemisphere.

The night before Midsummer Day, known as Midsummer Eve, is when celebrations traditionally begin; and this night has long been linked with otherworldly happenings, fairies, spirits, and mayhem. In Iceland, where the sun doesn't set at all during the solstice, it's said that on this night cows can speak, seals become human, and elves will show themselves to humans. Most stories, myths, and folk tales associated with the solstice are generally light-hearted and playful, as if drawing on this abundance of light and an excess of solar energy. At a time when the days are long and the landscape is full of colour and life, solstice celebrations are spirited, colourful, and full of fun.

# Sun Goddess of the Season

## SÓL

The Sun Goddess Sól was the guardian of the sun in Norse mythology. She travelled across the sky each day carrying the sun in a chariot drawn by two golden horses. Her horses were called Árvakr, meaning "early riser," and Alsviðr, meaning "swift", and they raced across the sky each day chased by Sköll, a wolf intent on catching them.

During the summer, with the long days of sunlight, Sól was considered to be outrunning the wolf, while in the winter as the days shortened the wolf was thought to be close by. Solar eclipses were believed to happen when Sköll got close to Sól, or even managed to briefly snap at her heels.

Similar to the Inca tradition there is also a sibling bond between the Norse moon and sun gods, but these roles are reversed; so while Sól guards the Sun, her brother Máni is the guardian of the Moon. Together Sól and Máni are destined to travel the skies continuously, to maintain the balance of light and dark, and to track the days and years for everyone on Earth below them.

Sól is most strongly associated with Midsummer, a time when the sun stays high in the sky and she is considered to be at her most powerful in her battle with the wolf Sköll.

# 10 Modern Rituals to Welcome the Summer

This Midsummer festival is all about celebrating the peak of the sun's energy, so it's a wonderful excuse to make the most of the long hours of sunlight, gather friends together, and celebrate outdoors.

Your celebrations can be as simple or elaborate as you like. You can choose to just bring in some summer flowers and herbs and quietly welcome the dawn, or you can stay up all night and throw a wild Midsummer party, if you feel like it. Whatever you decide to do, have a wonderful day and make the most of all that amazing solar energy.

At the moment in the year when the sun is at its full strength and the natural world is at its peak, here are a few ways to bring some solstice rituals into your home.

A WONDERFUL
EXCUSE TO TAKE
ADVANTAGE
OF THE LONG
HOURS OF
SUNLIGHT,
GATHER FRIENDS
TOGETHER,
AND CELEBRATE
OUTDOORS

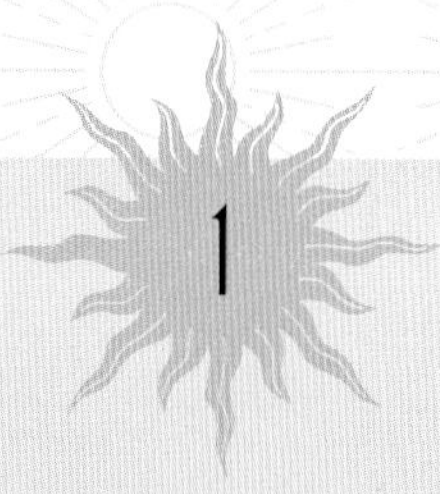

# GREET THE DAWN WITH AN ANCIENT RITUAL

As we have at each of the solar festivals in this book, we will start the new solar season by greeting the sunrise on the morning of the solstice. At Midsummer however, there's an extra twist to our early morning ritual. Bathing in the first dew of Summer Solstice morning was traditionally thought to bring good luck and health for the year ahead and is woven through the folklore of cultures right across Europe.

Some believed walking barefoot in the dew as the Midsummer Eve turned to dawn would help you stay fit and healthy in the coming year, while others believed washing your face in the dew of Midsummer morning would ensure youth and beauty. Other variations include leaving a bowl out overnight to collect the dew or even rolling naked in it to ensure good health and fortune in the coming months. I'll leave it up to you to decide how enthusiastically you decide to throw yourself into this ritual.

Many people choose to forgo sleep completely on the shortest night of the year, and stay up all night in order to see the sun rise. Stonehenge is perhaps the most famous example of an ancient solstice monument that still acts as a gathering place today. The monument is opened for visitors especially on each of the four solar festivals, with many staying up all night to greet the dawn as it rises above the stones on the longest day of the year.

For those that can't make it, there is usually a live stream of the event on the English Heritage website, so you can watch it remotely. Or you can, of course, just tune into the solstice energy wherever in the world you happen to be. Set an alarm or leave your curtains open to allow the sun to wake you naturally on the shortest night of the year and as you do, offer thanks for everything this summer has brought you so far. And perhaps collect a little of the morning solstice dew, just for luck.

If you set intentions at the Spring Equinox sunrise, now is a good time to check in with those and see how they are unfolding. Is there anything you can do to refocus these goals, or are you happy with where you are? If you need to gently realign your path, the solstice sunrise is a powerful time to do this. As always, this is a time for positivity and good energy, so be kind with yourself and focus on what you have already achieved, as well as considering where you want to go in the months ahead.

## STRENGTHEN THE SUN'S POWER WITH A BONFIRE

As with the Winter Solstice, most Summer Solstice rituals centre around fire, usually a communal bonfire. These fires were traditionally lit for their protective powers and to celebrate and boost the sun's power for the rest of the growing season. Because, conversely, although the peak of summer is being celebrated, there is an awareness that after the solstice, the sun's strength will start to diminish as we begin the slow but steady turn towards the Autumn Equinox. Solstice fires used to be considered a way of kindling the sun's power to give it a boost for the remainder of the growing season.

Across Europe bonfires have been traditionally lit on top of hills at the solstice, either as a beacon to ward off any evil spirits or to celebrate the longest day. This need for the protection that fire affords could have partly come from needing crops and livestock to prosper in the coming months. It could also be because spirits and magic were believed to be potent at Midsummer and bonfires were considered to have a protective element. Jumping over bonfires is another tradition that the bravest may attempt at the solstice; possibly for luck, or for granting wishes.

Scandinavian countries in particular have a long history of celebrating the Summer Solstice, as their distance from the equator means they experience particularly dramatic changes in light levels at this time of year. Around the time of the Summer Solstice, the sun will barely set all night, so Scandinavians are able to hold their celebrations under the midnight sun. Outdoor fires take on a celebratory feel and many choose to stay outside all night around the bonfire on Solstice Eve to greet the early solstice dawn.

# LIGHT THE SHORTEST NIGHT WITH CANDLES

Midsummer Eve, or Solstice Eve, has traditionally been considered a time when magic and mischief is strong. To symbolically keep the sun shining through the shortest night of the year, and as a symbol of protection against any Midsummer magic, it was usual to keep a candle burning in your home from sundown on the eve of the solstice until sunrise on solstice morning.

Even if you don't stay awake all night, lighting a candle on the eve of the solstice is a symbolic way to honour the power of the sun and bring its warmth into your home. Beeswax candles are beautiful to light at the solstice as they bring the rich honeyed scent of summer with them and they cast a beautifully warm glow. You could also choose candles with a summery fragrance or carefully encircle your candles with herbs (being mindful of fire safety) for some Midsummer magic. Just make sure to extinguish them before you go to sleep.

## HAVE A MIDSUMMER FEAST OUTSIDE

These long days of Midsummer are the perfect time to host a summer garden party or to have a picnic outdoors and enjoy the long, light evenings. Traditional foods eaten at Midsummer are strawberries, new potatoes seasoned with fresh herbs, salmon, fresh bread, and honey. Elderflowers are at their peak at this time of year too, and these tiny star-shaped flowers with their summery scent are intrinsically linked to this festival, so elderflower cordial makes a lovely solstice drink.

This is a beautiful, relaxed time of year, so make your meal as simple as possible and keep its preparation uncomplicated. You could use herbs or fresh flowers to decorate place settings and dot candles along the table.

A small herb posy also makes a lovely Midsummer gift, and if you have a Midsummer party you could use these to decorate each place setting. Cut a small bunch of herbs, tie together with string, and attach a paper gift tag with a Midsummer message for your friends or guests and instructions on how to preserve them. When your guests get their posy home they can hang it up somewhere to dry, preserving a little of the scent and memories of Midsummer to take with them into the darker months.

# ASK FOR A WATER BLESSING

At this time of strong solar energy, you might need to balance things out by seeking out some water to counteract the summer heat. In many ancient cultures blessings were offered, and sought, near springs and natural water sources during the summer months. In the UK, well-dressing is a ritual that still continues today, particularly in the north of the country where, around the time of the solstice, wells and natural springs are decorated with beautiful and intricate offerings made from natural materials. It is thought this tradition has links back to Ancient Roman or Celtic traditions of water blessings and it has been adapted and developed over time.

Well-dressings are made by pressing natural materials such as flower petals, stones, leaves, and moss into natural clay to form a mosaic image which is left near the water source as an offering to Mother Nature or the water gods. They can be as elaborate or as simple as you like, or you could perform a simpler version of this by placing flowers, leaves, or natural offerings close to your local water spring, river, or lake.

You could also counter some of that high-summer energy and heat by taking a cool dip in some outdoor water at the solstice if you are able, and if it is safe to do so.

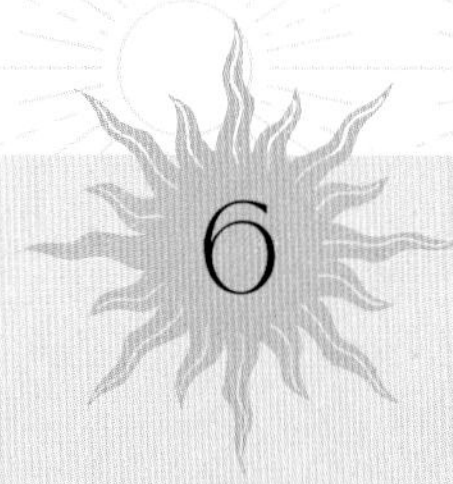

## GATHER AND DRY HERBS

With garden herbs at their peak, now is the time to cut and preserve them for use throughout the year. Herbs were believed by many to be at their most potent at Midsummer, and some cultures thought that herbs even acquired extra strong and magical healing powers on this day. Drying herbs at the height of the sun's power can help you preserve some of their strong solar energy, allowing you to take it with you into the autumn and winter.

Different herbs will lend themselves to different purposes, from culinary use to fragrances and decoration. If you plan to use your herbs for cooking, first ensure you are very certain of their identification and then clearly label them. Also check their properties to ensure they are suitable for eating. The same applies to herbs used for fragrance, as each herb has its own unique characteristics and properties, ranging from soothing to invigorating. Although a mixed bunch of herbs might look appealing, always pick and dry herbs separately, to ensure they retain their individual properties and avoid confusion at a later date.

Some of the herbs linked to this time of year are lavender, fennel, rosemary, mint, sage, and thyme.

Here are a few steps to follow to preserve your own herbs at Midsummer:

1. Pick your herbs in the morning, before the sun builds up too much heat but after any morning dew has evaporated.

2. Choose stems with healthy, intact leaves.

3. Cut herbs at the base of each individual stem and group them in small bunches of 5–10 (any more than this and they won't dry properly).

4. Use elastic bands to tie the herb bunches together (if you use string it will become loose as the herb stems dry out and shrink).

5. Ideally keep different herbs apart; don't mix bunches as they will be harder to separate when dry.

6. Hang the herbs up to dry somewhere warm but out of direct sunlight. Make sure there is good airflow and low moisture levels.

7. Give them a few weeks to thoroughly dry. When they feel crisp to the touch and a bit crumbly they're ready.

8. Strip the leaves from the stems and store them in clearly labelled airtight containers to keep them as fresh as possible for use in the coming autumn and winter.

9. Make a note on the outside of the jar, listing the qualities and properties of each herb along with the date you picked them.

# BAKE A MIDSUMMER CAKE

Fresh strawberries are at their peak in June, and as such, they have become synonymous with the Summer Solstice. In Scandinavian countries it's traditional to make a strawberry Midsummer cake to serve at solstice celebrations. This is a simple vanilla sponge cake layered up with fresh cream and topped with plenty of fresh strawberries, and it often takes centre stage in any outdoor celebrations.

There are so many other fresh, summery recipes to use up all those seasonal strawberries too: you could make strawberry jelly, strawberry cobbler, strawberry fool, strawberry salad, or of course, you could just enjoy them fresh with plenty of cream.

## MIDSUMMER STRAWBERRY CAKE

This is my version of a Midsummer cake, but you can adapt the recipe by decorating it any way you like. You could add strawberries to the filling instead of jam or you could add an extra layer of cream to the top. You could even add a sprinkling of edible flowers to decorate. The only non-negotiables are the cream and strawberries. It must contain these to be a traditional Midsummer cake!

### INGREDIENTS

- 175g (6oz) caster (superfine) sugar
- 175g (6oz) butter
- 3 eggs
- 5 drops vanilla essence
- 1½ tsp baking powder
- 175g (6oz) self-raising flour

**FOR THE FILLING AND TOPPING**

- Strawberry jam
- 200ml (7fl oz) whipping cream
- Fresh strawberries, sliced

## METHOD

**1.** Preheat the oven to 180°C/160°C fan/Gas 4 (350°F). Line two 20cm (8in) circular baking tins with baking (parchment) paper.

**2.** Combine the sugar, butter, eggs, vanilla essence, and baking powder in a bowl. Sift in the flour and mix well using a hand mixer or in a stand mixer until you get a smooth-textured batter.

**3.** Pour the batter into your lined cake tins.

**4.** Place in the centre of the oven and bake for 20 minutes or until they just start to turn a golden colour on top.

**5.** To test if your sponges are done, gently press the top of each cake – if it springs back up, it's done. If an indent remains, then cook for a few more minutes and test again.

**6.** Turn the cakes out onto a wire rack and allow to cool.

**7.** Once the cakes are cool, cover one of the sponges with a thin layer of strawberry jam.

**8.** Whisk your whipping cream with a hand mixer or in a stand mixer until it creates firm peaks (this is when it stands up in peaks without falling over).

**9.** Smooth a generous layer of whipped cream on top of the jam, then carefully place the second layer of sponge on top.

**10.** Top your cake with another layer of whipped cream and cover with sliced fresh strawberries. Serve immediately.

8

# TAKE A MIDSUMMER NIGHT'S DREAM

While some choose to stay awake all night on the shortest night, others use this magical night to predict the future, as the short nights have traditionally been a time of dreaming and fortune telling. In Scandinavian countries it's traditional to pick wild flowers at the solstice and place them under your pillow in order to dream of your future partner. The tradition is that if you pick seven different types of flower and place them under your pillow, your future partner will present themselves to you in your dreams.

Another variation is to place herbs under your pillow or near your bed on the eve of the solstice to influence your dreams. Different herbs were thought to have different qualities, so you could, in theory, influence your Midsummer dreaming by your careful choice of herbs.

The following herbs and flowers are all abundant at this time of year and have become associated with magic, love, and premonitions on Midsummer Eve. Before you use any herbs or botanicals be careful to educate yourself about their individual properties. Some botanicals can cause skin sensitivity when picked, others should be used in moderation, and many should never be ingested. If in doubt ask for professional advice.

## ST. JOHN'S WORT

This sunny-coloured herb has become deeply associated with this festival, thanks to its bright yellow flowers and an ancient belief in its magical properties at the solstice. Ideally it was considered fortuitous to gather it in the nude, and if you placed it under your pillow it was thought to protect against heartbreak.

## LAVENDER

This calming herb was frequently picked at the solstice and placed under a Midsummer pillow to ensure restful dreams: a much-needed quality on this feverish night of magic and mayhem. This cooling herb can counteract some of the heat of the solstice and it was also believed to keep bad spirits away and provide protection on this most magical of nights.

## CHAMOMILE

Known for its soothing and calming properties, chamomile has been connected with the sun for centuries. In Ancient Egypt it was thought to have been revered and even associated with the sun god Ra, possibly because of its close visual link to the sun with its golden central disc surrounded by ray-like petals.

## LADY'S BEDSTRAW

The sun-coloured flowers of this herb have a rich, honey scent that typifies Midsummer and were believed in some parts of Europe to have magical qualities and a connection to the fairies in Midsummer. As the name suggests, this fragrant herb was also used to fill mattresses in Medieval times, providing sweet-smelling dreams.

## ROSES

Roses are deeply associated with Midsummer and are linked to youth, beauty, and love at this time of year. If rose petals were picked on Midsummer eve and placed under a pillow, it was thought your true love would appear to you in your dreams.

# TAKE A SUMMER SOLSTICE NATURE WALK

At this time of year when daylight hours are at their peak, the pull to be outside feels irresistible. The Summer Solstice is an absolutely beautiful time, days are long and hot, and nights are short, and hot; everywhere is teeming with life and activity.

If you've been taking mindful walks at each of the solstices and equinoxes, you might want to take the same route for this walk, as the difference since your last walk at the Spring Equinox is likely to be dramatic.

## WHAT YOU MIGHT SPOT

June is a month that crackles with life; hedgerows thicken up, grass grows at a terrific rate, flowers jostle for space in the garden. Roses fill the air with thick summer perfume and it's the peak season for tomatoes, strawberries, and raspberries in the allotment. Trees will be sporting their thick summer canopy, now creating much-needed shade underneath. Hedgerows, verges, and field edges will have filled out too, creating a tangled screen of wildflowers and foliage alongside paths and roads. Everything will be looking lush, green, and very *alive*.

The Summer Solstice is also a beautifully noisy time to be outdoors, with wildlife making the most of the warm conditions. Any birds that were born in the spring will be fledging from their nests now, testing their wings and cautiously seeking independence as their parents watch them carefully from nearby. For early risers, the dawn chorus should still be going strong in June too, as songbirds take advantage of the still early morning air to broadcast their message loud and clear. The gentle drone of bees busily working away is a soundtrack to the summer for many, and there's an explosion of insect life at this time, too.

The opportunity to be out later in the hot evenings also gives us a wonderful opportunity to see nocturnal animals. The trick is to sit quietly outside as dusk falls and allow yourself to gently settle into the warmth of the evening, becoming a tiny part of the landscape all around you. If you're lucky, you might see bats fly overhead as they venture out in the warm evening air to catch insects. Pure summer magic.

## UPDATE YOUR SEASONAL SHELF

It's time to update your seasonal collection, or nature altar, to reflect the new season. At this time of year there are so many beautiful things to find outdoors and add to your display. You might like to bring in fresh flowers and herbs and arrange them alongside a sunshine-coloured candle. You might also include something that reminds you of the sun at this pivotal moment in the solar year: a decoration, ornament, or illustration. As always, the beauty of a seasonal shelf or altar is that no two will be the same; yours will be completely bespoke and personal to you, so make sure to fill yours with things that bring you joy.

If you're helping children to make their own nature table, you might want to help them to make a display with some orange, yellow, or gold-coloured silks, sun shapes, or summer animals, alongside some illustrated books that explain the festival of the solstice, and a representation of the sun. You could also include an illustration of a sunflower or daisy, as these are beautiful examples of summer flowers that move their heads to follow the sun from east to west over the course of a day.

If you need some ideas to help you get started with your own seasonal shelf, or nature table, for the Summer Solstice you might like to bring in some of the following items:

- A vase of fresh garden flowers.
- A small bunch of fresh herbs. When picked at Midsummer, many herbs are thought to be at their most potent, so this is a good time to harvest and preserve their magic.
- Seasonal books that tap into the light, heat, and magic of Midsummer.
- A decoration, drawing, or ornament that represents the sun.
- A sweet-smelling yellow beeswax candle.
- Images or words that represent the Summer Solstice to you. These could include a postcard from a place that is special to you, a favourite poem or a quote that signifies to you all the best things about summer.
- A small dish or container of cool water to counterbalance the strong solar energy of the solstice.

# Summer Solstice Crafts

## FLOWER AND HERB CROWN

Flowers are in abundance now and herbs are believed by many to be at their most potent at Midsummer, so this is a good time to gather and preserve them or to pick them fresh to weave into crowns or wreaths. Flower crowns were traditionally worn for Midsummer celebrations in Scandinavian countries, where garlands of flowers and herbs were made and worn to ward off mischievous spirits. You could also repurpose this as a wreath for your front door to protect against solstice magic once you've finished wearing it.

**YOU WILL NEED**

- Wire
- Scissors
- Fresh greenery
- Selection of freshly cut herbs (woody herbs such as rosemary and lavender work best)
- Florist tape
- Selection of seasonal flowers

### HERE'S HOW TO MAKE YOUR OWN FLOWER AND HERB CROWN

**1.** Measure the circumference of your head and cut a piece of wire the same size, adding a little extra at the ends, then bend into a circle as the base for your wreath and twist the ends together. If you're using thin wire you may want to wrap it around a few times to make a sturdier base.

**2.** Take small pieces of your greenery and herbs and attach one by one to the wire base with the florist tape. Affix the stems with the tape and leave the ends loose so they stand away from the crown.

**3.** Repeat until the wire is covered with a layer of greenery.

**4.** Next take your flowers and bunch them into mini bouquets of 3 flowers each. Tie them together at the stem with florist tape.

**5.** Take each mini bouquet and add it to the crown, securing with a little tape.

**6.** Vary the size and colour of the flowers as you go to create a wild effect rather than anything too rigid and neat. Have fun with your design.

**7.** Wear and enjoy!

**Note:** As you're using fresh flowers, this crown will need to be made shortly before you plan to wear it and it won't last much past Midsummer night. All the leaves and flowers can be removed and composted once you've finished with it. The wire base can be kept for next year.

## SOLSTICE PRESSED FLOWER LANTERNS

These are the sister lanterns to the ones we made at the Autumn Equinox and they are bright, pretty and twinkly: the perfect decoration for the night of Midnight Sun. You'll need to press your flowers first to preserve them, but if you do this in advance, the lantern itself takes only a short while to make, and a cluster of them would make the perfect centrepiece for a solstice party. If you're really short on time you can buy sheets of pre-pressed flowers to use for this.

**YOU WILL NEED**

- Glass jar(s)
- Clear-drying craft glue (such as PVA)
- Paintbrush
- Pressed flowers (see tip)
- Tealights (candle or battery powered)

### HERE'S HOW TO MAKE YOUR OWN FLOWER LANTERN

**1.** Take your clean glass jar(s) and apply a thin layer of craft glue to the outside with your paintbrush. (Old jam jars are perfect for this, and if you're making several lanterns, then a mix of different sizes and shapes is fine and looks very pretty on a table. Just make sure to thoroughly wash all the jars before you start.)

**2.** Add your pressed flowers and leaves to the outside of the jar(s). Do not worry about symmetry here – a mix of colours and shapes scattered across the glass, with some petals overlapping, actually works better than a careful symmetrical pattern. Think wild and organic.

**3.** When you have finished, apply a thin layer of glue over the top of the flowers to seal them.

**4.** Allow to dry completely.

**5.** Add a tealight to each lantern and use them to decorate your solstice night.

**Tip:** Before you start you'll need to have pressed your flowers in advance. You can buy pre-pressed flowers, but it doesn't take a minute to press your own: just take a selection of small flowers and leaves and press them flat between two pieces of absorbent paper. Place them in a flower press or under a few heavy books and put them somewhere warm until they are completely dry, which could take around 2 weeks. Choose small flowers for this, or if using larger flowers like roses, press individual flower petals instead.

# MIDSUMMER DREAM PILLOW

If you want to try a little solstice-night dreaming, this herb pillow will help to scent your dreams. It's really quick to make and involves no sewing, so it can be made at speed on Midsummer Eve. You could make these with friends if you're having a solstice party.

**YOU WILL NEED**

- About 25 x 25cm (10 x 10in) square of natural fabric (thin cotton or linen will work best)
- Dried herbs or flowers with soothing properties (e.g. lavender, rose petals, chamomile flowers; remember to check the herbs' properties)
- String or ribbon

**HERE'S HOW TO MAKE YOUR OWN MIDSUMMER DREAM PILLOW**

**1.** Take your square of fabric and place a couple of teaspoons of your chosen dried herbs in the centre.

**2.** Fold the bottom edge of fabric up over the herbs.

**3.** Fold in each of the sides.

**4.** Fold the top down, as if you are making an envelope to enclose the herbs.

**5.** Once the herbs are safely tucked inside, tie the flat parcel with string or ribbon.

**6.** You should now have a small flat envelope filled with sweet, dream-inducing herbs, the perfect size to slip under a pillow or inside a pillowcase.

Place it under your pillow or inside your pillowcase just before you go to bed. Or if you are very sensitive to scent, just pop it under your pillow a couple of hours before you go to bed instead, then remove it before you go to sleep.

Enjoy your Midsummer dream!

# PAPER SUN DECORATION

These folded paper suns would be perfect to decorate a summer solstice party. All you need are a few sheets of tissue paper and card and a glue stick to create pretty, reusable decorations in half an hour. They can also fold down neatly after use to be stored away until the next party. Hang them up above a table or in a window to welcome the sun and your guests.

### YOU WILL NEED

- Yellow, orange, or gold tissue paper (1 large sheet of 50 x 75cm/20 x 30in will make 2 decorations)
- Ruler
- Scissors
- String
- Glue stick
- Sheet of A5 card

### HERE'S HOW TO MAKE YOUR OWN PAPER SUN DECORATION

**1.** Cut the tissue paper into a 75 x 20cm (30 x 8in) strip.

**2.** Starting with the short edge, fold over a 2cm (¾in) strip.

**3.** Flip the tissue paper over and fold another a 2cm (¾in) strip.

**4.** Repeat this process, alternating sides until you've folded up all the tissue paper into a concertina-style stack that is 20cm (8in) long and 2cm (¾in) wide.

**5.** Fold this stack of tissue paper in half widthways, unfold again, and tie a small length of string around the centre crease.

**6.** Fold the stack back in half and glue the two middle sections together.

**7.** From the card cut two strips of 15 x 1cm (6 x ⅜in).

**8.** Glue these to either side of the folded paper stack.

**9.** Holding these card strips, gently unfold the paper fan to create a fluted circle.

**10.** Carefully poke a hole through the top of the cardboard strips, then thread a piece of string through these holes and tie.

**Note:** After use, these decorations can be carefully folded back down to store flat, and reused later.

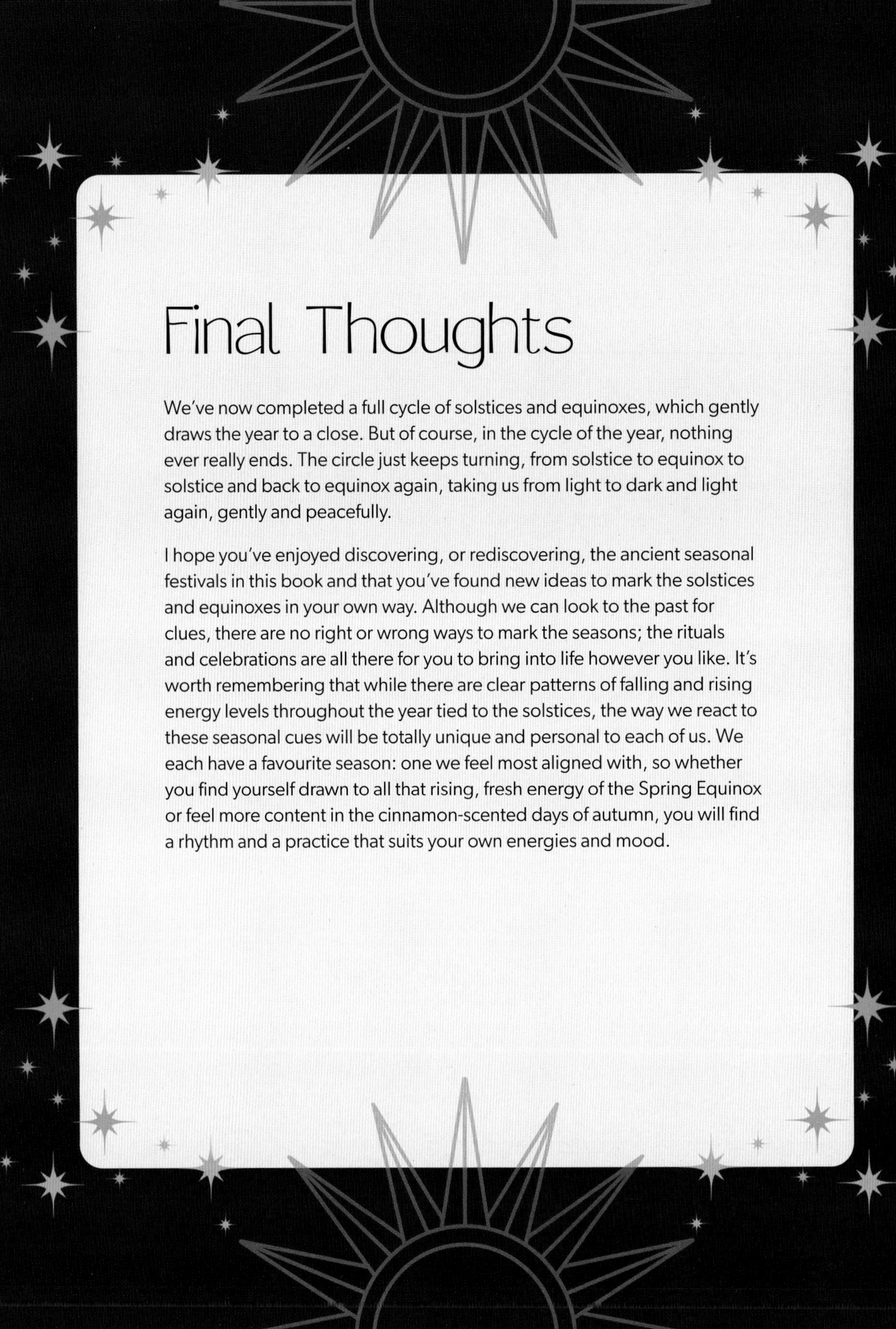

# Final Thoughts

We've now completed a full cycle of solstices and equinoxes, which gently draws the year to a close. But of course, in the cycle of the year, nothing ever really ends. The circle just keeps turning, from solstice to equinox to solstice and back to equinox again, taking us from light to dark and light again, gently and peacefully.

I hope you've enjoyed discovering, or rediscovering, the ancient seasonal festivals in this book and that you've found new ideas to mark the solstices and equinoxes in your own way. Although we can look to the past for clues, there are no right or wrong ways to mark the seasons; the rituals and celebrations are all there for you to bring into life however you like. It's worth remembering that while there are clear patterns of falling and rising energy levels throughout the year tied to the solstices, the way we react to these seasonal cues will be totally unique and personal to each of us. We each have a favourite season: one we feel most aligned with, so whether you find yourself drawn to all that rising, fresh energy of the Spring Equinox or feel more content in the cinnamon-scented days of autumn, you will find a rhythm and a practice that suits your own energies and mood.

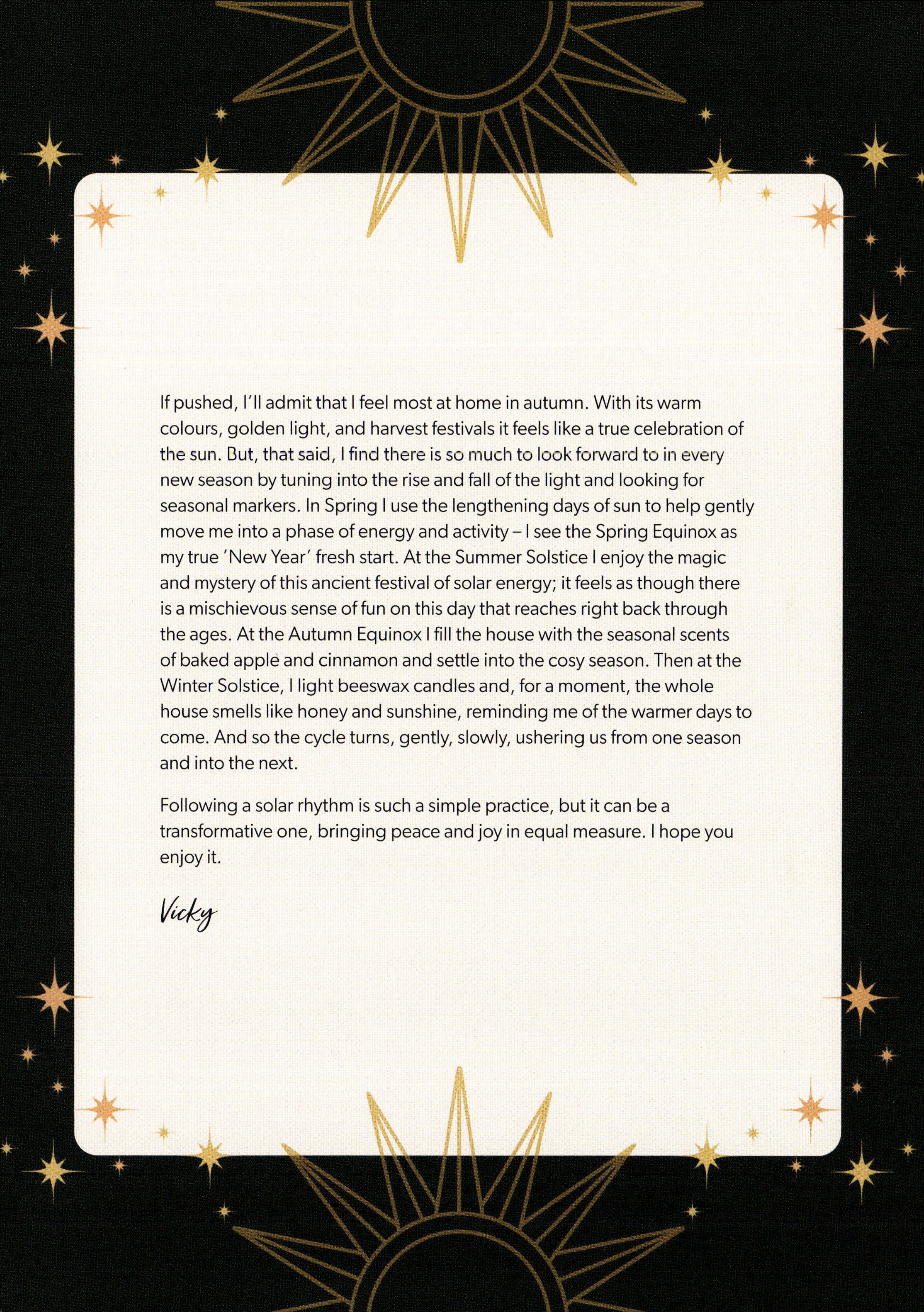

If pushed, I'll admit that I feel most at home in autumn. With its warm colours, golden light, and harvest festivals it feels like a true celebration of the sun. But, that said, I find there is so much to look forward to in every new season by tuning into the rise and fall of the light and looking for seasonal markers. In Spring I use the lengthening days of sun to help gently move me into a phase of energy and activity – I see the Spring Equinox as my true 'New Year' fresh start. At the Summer Solstice I enjoy the magic and mystery of this ancient festival of solar energy; it feels as though there is a mischievous sense of fun on this day that reaches right back through the ages. At the Autumn Equinox I fill the house with the seasonal scents of baked apple and cinnamon and settle into the cosy season. Then at the Winter Solstice, I light beeswax candles and, for a moment, the whole house smells like honey and sunshine, reminding me of the warmer days to come. And so the cycle turns, gently, slowly, ushering us from one season and into the next.

Following a solar rhythm is such a simple practice, but it can be a transformative one, bringing peace and joy in equal measure. I hope you enjoy it.

*Vicky*

# Further Reading

## BOOKS

*The Stations of the Sun: A History of the Ritual Year in Britain* by Ronald Hutton

*The World's Heritage: The Definitive Guide to all World Heritage Sites* by UNESCO

*The World of Stonehenge* by Duncan Garrow and Neil Wilkin

*Newgrange, Knowth & Dowth: Exploring the Majestic Passage Tombs of Ancient Ireland* by Liam Mac Uistin

*Telling the Seasons: Stories, Celebrations and Folklore Around the Year* by Martin Maudsley

*Tales of the Night Sky: Stories of Stars from Around the World* by Corinna Keefe

*The Shortest Day* by Susan Cooper

*What to Look For in Spring, What to Look For in Summer, What to Look For in Autumn and What to Look For in Winter* by Elizabeth Jenner

## WEBSITES

Unesco (ancient solar monuments on the World Heritage List) – **whc.unesco.org**

English Heritage – **www.english-heritage.org.uk**

Met Office (solstices, equinoxes and seasons) – **www.metoffice.gov.uk**

Time and Date (solstice and equinox dates) – **www.timeanddate.com**

The Old Farmer's Almanac – **www.almanac.com**

The Woodland Trust (seasonal wildlife and nature craft) – **www.woodlandtrust.org.uk/blog**

The NHS (Vitamin D and Seasonal Affective Disorder) – **www.nhs.uk**

## APPS AND PODCASTS

*Solstice* – a free app showing how much daylight there is each day

*The Ancients* podcast – History Hit, hosted by Tristan Hughes

*The English Heritage* podcast – Charles Rowe

# About the Author

Victoria Harrison is a lifestyle journalist and stylist, and the author of *Rewild Your Home: Bring the Outside In and Live Well Through Nature* and *Happy by Design: How to Create a Home That Boosts Your Health and Happiness*.

Victoria has written for many leading magazines and newspapers over the past 20 years. She specializes in seasonal living and how a connection to the natural world can help to bring us peace and happiness.

Learn more and sign up to Victoria's Seasonal Living newsletter at www.vickyharrison.com or victoriaharrison.substack.com.

# Acknowledgements

Many thanks to my agent Fiona Lindsay, for understanding the concept of this book as soon as I pitched it and for patiently searching for the right home for it.

A huge thank you to everyone at David & Charles: Lizzie Kaye for seeing the potential and helping to shape it, Victoria Allen and Claire Rogers for patient editing, Sam Staddon for the beautiful design and Lauren Spooner for the lovely illustrations.

And finally a big thank you to the members of my Seasonal Living newsletter community. The ideas in this book came to life thanks to your supportive encouragement. This book is for you.

# Index

A VERBENA BOOK


Verbena is an imprint of David and Charles Ltd, Suite A, Tourism House, Pynes Hill, Exeter, EX2 5WS



First published in the UK and USA in 2025



A catalogue record for this book is available from the British Library.

ISBN-13: 9781446316382 paperback
ISBN-13: 9781446316399 EPUB

This book has been printed on paper from approved suppliers and made from pulp from sustainable sources.

Printed in China through Asia Pacific Offset for:
David and Charles, Ltd
Suite A, Tourism House, Pynes Hill, Exeter, EX2 5WS

10 9 8 7 6 5 4 3 2 1

Publishing Director: Ame Verso
Senior Commissioning Editor: Lizzie Kaye
Publishing Manager: Jeni Chown
Editor: Victoria Allen
Copy Editor: Claire Rogers
Design: Sam Staddon
Pre-press Designer: Susan Reansbury
Illustrations: Lauren Spooner
Production Manager: Beverley Richardson

David and Charles publishes high-quality books on a wide range of subjects. For more information visit www.davidandcharles.com.

Follow us on Instagram by searching for @verbena_books and @dandcbooks.

Layout of the digital edition of this book may vary depending on reader hardware and display settings.

**Safety Note:** This book contains some advice on using herbs. Please be aware that some people with allergies, who are pregnant or breastfeeding, or have underlying health conditions, may need to take care when it comes to using certain herbs. If you are unsure, ask a doctor or health professional for advice.